Seeking the Mystical Child

Seeking the Mystical Child: Nurturing Young Children's Identity, Faith, and Belief by Danette Littleton and Meryl Sole is a unique book that presents insights into children's unnoticed spiritual worlds. The authors acquired voices and portraits of children from differing cultures through qualitative research. Interpretations of ancient and contemporary Judaism, Christianity, and Islam provided context. This book is for those who desire to understand children's lived experiences, seen and unseen, of wonder, awe, and purity of heart. Seekers of meaning in the lives of children may find meaning for themselves in *Seeking the Mystical Child: Nurturing Young Children's Identity, Faith, and Belief.*

Danette Littleton earned a Ph.D. at the University of Texas-Austin. She is a retired professor of music education and a former music teacher for children in elementary and preschool. Research studies on children's spontaneous play with music were presented at national and international conferences and universities. Her work is published in journals, book chapters, papers, and the books *When Music Goes to School: Perspectives on Learning and Teaching* and *Knowing the Children We Teach: Essays on Music Learning* (with co-author Meryl Sole), and children's books, *Side by Side: A Friendship in Black and White* and *Side by Side With New Friends.*

Meryl Sole earned an Ed.D. from Teacher's College, Columbia University. Musical studies in music history, theory, and French horn performance prepared her for a career in higher education, teaching graduate and undergraduate courses in music education at New York University and Teacher's College, Columbia University. Her research focuses on early childhood music development, toddlers' spontaneous crib songs, and musical parenting. Her work was presented at numerous national and international conferences and published in *Psychology of Music* and the *Oxford Handbook of Early Childhood Music Learning and Development.* She co-authored *Knowing the Children We Teach* with Danette Littleton.

Other Eye on Education Books
Available from Routledge
(www.routledge.com/eyeoneducation)

A New Vision for Early Childhood
Rethinking Our Relationships with Young Children
Noah Hichenberg

Reimagining the Role of Teachers in Nature-based Learning
Helping Children be Curious, Confident, and Caring
Rachel Larimore and Claire Warden

Teaching Higher-Order Thinking to Young Learners, K–3
How to Develop Sharp Minds for the Disinformation Age
Steffen Saifer

Seeking the Mystical Child
Nurturing Young Children's Identity, Faith, and Belief

Danette Littleton and Meryl Sole

Designed cover image: David Litchfield

First published 2026
by Routledge
605 Third Avenue, New York, NY 10158

and by Routledge
4 Park Square, Milton Park, Abingdon, Oxon, OX14 4RN

Routledge is an imprint of the Taylor & Francis Group, an informa business

© 2026 Taylor & Francis

The right of Danette Littleton and Meryl Sole to be identified as authors of this work has been asserted in accordance with sections 77 and 78 of the Copyright, Designs and Patents Act 1988.

All rights reserved. No part of this book may be reprinted or reproduced or utilised in any form or by any electronic, mechanical, or other means, now known or hereafter invented, including photocopying and recording, or in any information storage or retrieval system, without permission in writing from the publishers.

Trademark notice: Product or corporate names may be trademarks or registered trademarks, and are used only for identification and explanation without intent to infringe.

ISBN: 978-1-032-76225-8 (hbk)
ISBN: 978-1-032-75890-9 (pbk)
ISBN: 978-1-003-47765-5 (ebk)

DOI: 10.4324/9781003477655

Typeset in Palatino
by SPi Technologies India Pvt Ltd (Straive)

When God wanted to experience what he created, He hid in the human heart.

—*a Sufi saying*

Contents

Gratitude viii
Meet the Authors ix
Remembrance xi

Introduction 1

1 The Wondering Child 8

2 The Spiritual Child 14

3 The Natural Child 23

4 The Mystical Child 29

5 Framing Portraits 36

6 Pilgrimage 45

7 One With God 57

8 Children of Faith 71

9 Peace in Search of Makers 77

10 Seeking God 83

11 The Mystery of God 93

12 Spiritual Engagements: Activities and Experiences 99

13 Spiritual Sojourners 107

Thanks to the children and teachers who contributed to our work and family and friends who supported us.

Meet the Authors

Danette Littleton
University of Texas at Austin, PhD
Florida State University, MME. & BME

Musical studies in piano, voice, and choral conducting led to a career in music education, where I taught students from preschool through high school and university. As a Professor of Music Education, I prepared music teachers for positions in public and private schools. I designed music and arts education programs funded by the National Endowment for the Arts, the Getty Foundation, the Wolf Trap Institute for Early Learning in the Arts, Head Start, Sesame Street Workshop, the Leonard Bernstein Center, the Gibson Guitar Corporation, the Grammy Foundation, and the Lifelong Learning Society. I was invited to develop a music therapy program for cancer survivors and their families, to give lectures at churches and temples on music and spirituality, and to present research at conferences and universities in the United States, Canada, England, Japan, Korea, Sweden, and South Africa. Publications: *When Music Goes to School: Perspectives on Learning and Teaching*, and, for children, *Side by Side* and *Side by Side with New Friends*. Also *Knowing the Children We Teach: Essays on Music Learning* and *Seeking the Mystical Child: Nurturing Young Children's Identity, Faith, and Belief* with Meryl Sole.

Meryl Sole
Teacher's College, Columbia University, Doctorate in Music and Music Education, Ed.D., Ed.M
Boston University, Masters in French Horn Performance, MM

Musical training in music history, theory, and French horn performance led me to a career as a music teacher at the university level and in preschools. As an Adjunct Professor of Music at Teachers College and New York University, I teach undergraduate and graduate students in music education and research. Full-time music faculty positions at The University of New Haven, Bergen Community College, and SUNY Empire State College. Additional teaching at Fordham University, Adelphi University, and New Jersey City University. My research has been published in peer-reviewed journals and books, and I have presented my work at national and international conferences. My research focuses on early childhood music, where I explore musical parenting and musical development through toddlers' spontaneous "crib songs." I also study popular music and creative approaches in music theory pedagogy. Recent publications include articles in *Psychology of Music* and *The Journal for Popular Music Education*. Book chapters are featured in *The Oxford Handbook of Early Childhood Music Learning and Development* and Oxford University Press' *Teaching Instrumental Music: Contemporary Perspectives and Pedagogies*. Two books, *Knowing the Children We Teach: Essays on Music Learning* and *Seeking the Mystical Child: Nurturing Young Children's Identity, Faith, and Belief*, are co-authored with Danette Littleton.

Remembrance

Janice Harper Smith
1941–2024

> From childhood, Janice and I became lifelong friends, two friends with one soul that neither time nor space nor death can overcome.
>
> –Danette

Introduction

Danette Littleton and Meryl Sole

The goal of this book concerns our interests in children's beingness, who they know themselves to be. We seek a deeper understanding of children's beliefs about themselves and others and the meaning they ascribe to lived phenomena in their known world.

Peering into children's ways of knowing is a delicate task, for theirs is a world apart of secret places, intimacy, mystery, and dreams. Van Manen and Levering (1996) said,

> …the experience of the secret place as a sacred place may spiritualize the child. It may let us experience at the core of our being the sacred impulse for the free formation of the self, the experimentation with personal being and becoming.
>
> (25)

In private spaces, closets and attics, trees and thickets, children are free to wonder at peace and alone. Van Manen and Levering suggest that "… as adults, we may at times still long for this secret place and seek it in adventures of solitude so as to renew ourselves in a self-creating process" (25).

In our previous book, *Knowing the Children We Teach: Essays on Music Learning* (2023), we explored the interconnected lives of children with their music teachers in classroom settings. At the outset, we surmised that music teachers are educated on *what* to teach about music and are prepared with teaching methods but must be made aware of *who* they teach. We proposed ways music teachers might better understand their students' lives within and outside the classroom. Specifically, we asked if there were prevailing associations in children's music and spiritual experiences. Teacher interviews, data collection, and analysis yielded distinctive themes, such as goodness and care for others, wonderment and imagination, and individualization.

The present book seeks to expand our understanding of spirituality in children's lives. At the outset, our scholarship searches specific to children's spirituality revealed that it is the least-studied attribute of children's lived experiences. Recently, interest in spirituality as a core component of child development has gained attention across disciplines such as psychology, sociology, anthropology, and religion.

Philosophers, theologians, and seekers of life's meaning have studied or mused about the human spirit and its power for transcendence throughout time and civilizations. The general literature on the nature of spirituality shows that, conceptually, spirituality has many meanings. Philip Sheldrake, religious historian, theologian, and leading scholar in the interdisciplinary field of spirituality, offers a clear-minded and succinct frame of reference. In *A Brief History of Spirituality* (2007), he writes:

> In her classic work, *Mysticism*, Evelyn Underhill (1955) suggests that human beings are vision-creating beings rather than merely tool-making animals. They are driven by goals that are more than mere physical perfection or intellectual supremacy. Humans desire what might be called spiritual fulfillment. For this reason, an enduring interest in spirituality should not surprise us. Yet despite its fuzziness, it is possible to suggest that the word "spirituality" refers to the deepest values and meanings by which people seek to live. In other words, "spirituality"

implies some vision of the human spirit and of what will assist it to achieve its full potential

(1)

In his groundbreaking work, *The Spiritual Lives of Children* (1991), Robert Coles, a child psychologist, conducted over five hundred interviews with children from Christian, Jewish, Muslim religions, and secular traditions. In addition to conducting interviews, Coles collected children's drawings that expressed their experience of religion and spirituality. His methodology departed from studies of cognitive inquiry in the Piagetian tradition; instead, Coles approached children directly by listening to their stories. Coles believed that studies of intellectual comprehension conducted in a structured setting needed to be revised to investigate children's ways of knowing, experiencing, and expressing personal thoughts. Coles explained, "The point is that I let the children know as clearly as possible, and as often as necessary, what it is I am trying to learn, how they can help me" (27).

David Hay and Rebecca Nye conducted significant inquiries concerning children's spirituality. In *The Spirit of the Child* (1998/2006), they explored the distinction between religion and spirituality within theological, social, and political complexities. The authors defined categories of spiritual sensitivities and provided informative guidelines for their studies (59). Hay offered the following qualities: a) Awareness sensing, characterized by the here and now, flow and focusing; b) Mystery sensing, including wonder, awe, and imagination; and c) Value sensing, according to delight and despair, goodness, and meaning. In the Hay and Nye studies, children's narratives were recorded, transcribed, and analyzed according to questions embedded in the established categories.

To understand the wonder-filled experiences in children's lives of reality and imagination, I examined Edward Robinson's work, *The Original Vision* (1977). He asserted that the original vision of childhood is often forgotten. Despite such neglect, he proposed that the memory of childhood experiences remains, and may be rediscovered in adulthood if prompted. Robinson offered his understanding of the influence of childhood in the lives of children and adults.

In a recent work by Tobin Hart, *The Secret Spiritual World of Children* (2010), he wrote,

> We will explore five general kinds of spiritual capacities: wisdom, wonder, wondering, the meeting of you and me, and seeing the invisible. These may even emerge as a spiritual temperament – the style or styles through which the child's spirituality most naturally flows
>
> (10)

When studying children, we enter their worlds as travelers and whisperers, treading with quiet footsteps. Having long lost the innocence of wonder by the practicalities of living and schooling, we struggle to find entrance to our once-upon-a-time childhood. Listen to Charles de Lint, from one of his many books for children and youth,

> It's easy to believe in magic when you're young. Anything you couldn't explain was magic then. It didn't matter if it was science or a fairy tale. Electricity and elves were both infinitely mysterious and equally possible—elves probably more so.

Children, like artists and clowns, dreamers and alchemists, seek that which is not what it seems to be. To reignite our openness to wonder, awe, and enchantment, we need a paradigm shift in how we seek to understand children's inner lives.

In our search to better understand children's spirituality, Dr. Sole observed children engaged in the many languages of music, dance, visual arts, make-believe play, drama, and story. She invited children aged from 4 to 10 of different faiths and non-faith traditions to participate in arts activities according to simple themes of natural and unknown worlds. We surmised that selected prompts and settings would encourage children's imagination without prescribing or directing their responses. Studies of children's free play with music (Littleton, 1991) show that it requires settings for children to explore and create without instruction or adult intervention.

In an exploratory study, Dr. Sole invited a preschool teacher to provide her 3- and 4-year-old students opportunities to listen to the music of four spiritual traditions: Judaism, Hinduism, Christianity, and Native American. She offered the children this prompt: "Listen and show how the music feels to you." Once a week over three weeks, children were provided poster-sized art paper, markers, and crayons in an open space for moving. The children responded without previous information about the origins of the music, musicians, and instruments. The teacher unobtrusively observed the children as they listened, made drawings, and freely moved. Quietly, she took notes whenever children made comments. At the end of each week, Dr. Sole collected the teacher's notes, the children's drawings, and movement videos for analysis.

In the beginning, some children displayed remarkable intuition, drawing images representing the music. For example, while listening to the Hebrew prayer *Hashkivenu*, many children drew pictures of families and safe homes. While the children did not understand the translation of the Hebrew prayer, they understood the feeling of seeking God's protection and comfort. One child described her drawing by saying, "This is my family in our house. We don't let the bad guys in." As the sessions continued, Dr. Sole noticed that some children seemed less focused on the music and that their drawings seemed unrelated or incongruous. Perhaps the activity was too abstract for children this young. However, on the final day of the study, a video revealed a little boy, Max, deeply immersed in the music, as if in a transcendent state—a mystical child. This is a narrative of the video.

The children are scattered about the room, some seated, some standing. Each has an oversized piece of brown butcher-block paper and markers, crayons, and colored pencils. The recording begins as female voices chant, "Yo way yo, yo way yo way, Yo way yo hi ya, yo way yo hi ya." A pair of boys chatter and imitate the singing, a girl twirls like a ballerina, and children scatter about. The room is chaotic and busy. One little boy in a long-sleeved brown shirt stands off to the side. His movements begin slowly in his wrist and quickly flow through his entire body. Classmates surround him, but he is in his world. He moves gracefully as the music takes over his body, arms and legs swaying, spinning, and floating. His teacher immediately notices Max, remarking that he is "solitary and seems transfixed" in what she called "a dreamy state." The children ask to hear the song again. Max makes his way to a table with art materials as the music continues. He embodies the music and, with eyes closed, uses his yellow crayon to dance back and forth on the paper, changing motion in sync with the tempo and dynamics. Later, Max remarks, "I feel relaxed. The tune makes me calm."

Our investigation of children's experience of spirituality required a phenomenological approach. The elusive nature of this inquiry suggests that the interpretation and meaning we ascribe to our findings may need closer scrutiny. Still, we assert that they are generative and presume implications for learning and teaching. Phenomenological methods differ from quantitative methods, which utilize a controlled set of procedures to obtain verifiable conclusions about the phenomena. Instead, "the purpose of inquiry in the human sciences was understanding (*verstehen*) rather than proof or prediction" (Frederick Erikson, in *A History of Qualitative Inquiry in Social and Education Research*, 2011, 43).

While no one method of inquiry concerning human nature is all-inclusive, cultural anthropology methods, including, but not limited to, participant-observer and non-participant observer, are most appropriate to the study of children's spiritual awareness. In his book, *Writing in the Dark: Phenomenological Studies in Interpretive Inquiry* (2016), Max Van Manen writes, "From a philosophical perspective, it is not at all surprising that wonder is the central methodological feature of phenomenological inquiry, since phenomenology is a physical project. ... Phenomenology not only finds its starting point in wonder, [but] it must also induce wonder" (5).

These inquiries concerned young children's experience of spirituality as they engage in music, dance, image, and story. Listening to children and observing them in sacred and secular places and natural settings revealed their unfettered enchantment, awe, and wonder. Even when adults were present, we noted that children acted alone as if in a private world, thus adding to our understanding of children's spiritual worlds.

References

Coles, Robert. *The Spiritual Life of Children*. Houghton Mifflin, 1991.

Erikson, Frederick. "A History of Qualitative Inquiry in Social and Educational Research." *The Sage Handbook of Qualitative Research* (2011), 4, pp.43–59.

Hart, Tobin. *The Secret Spiritual World of Children: The Breakthrough Discovery That Profoundly Alters Our Conventional Views of Children's Mystical Experiences*. New World Library, 2010.

Hay, Daniel, and Rebecca Nye. *The Spirit of the Child*. Jessica Kingsley Publishers, 2006.

Littleton, Danette. *Influence of Play Settings on Preschool Children's Music and Play Behaviors*. University of Texas at Austin, 1991.

Littleton, Danette, and Meryl Sole. *Knowing the Children We Teach: Essays on Music Learning*. Rowman & Littlefield, 2023.

Robinson, Edward. *The Original Vision: A Study of the Religious Experience of Childhood*. Seabury Press, 1977.

Sheldrake, Philip. *A Brief History of Spirituality*. John Wiley and Sons, 2007.

Underhill, Evelyn. *Mysticism: A Study in the Nature and Development of Man's Spiritual Consciousness*. Meridian Books, 1955.

Van Manen, Max *Writing in the Dark: Phenomenological Studies in Interpretive Inquiry*. Routledge, 2016.

Van Manen, Max, and Bas Levering. *Childhood Secrets: Intimacy, Privacy, and the Self Reconsidered*. Teachers College Press, 1996.

1

The Wondering Child

Danette Littleton

Children wonder about many big things, such as, "Where was I before I was born?" When adults offer answers like "Well, Mommy and I created you," young children might not be satisfied. Instead, they seek more, the unseen, unnamed, and unknown.

> Gazing at the night sky, the child asks,
> "What is that?"
>
> The parent answers, "It's a meteor that burns up when it reaches the earth's atmosphere, a star."
>
> Child, "A dying star?"
>
> "Some call them shooting stars because they move so fast and disappear."
>
> Child, "Is it a wishing star?"
> "It can be. You know the song *When You Wish Upon a Star?*"
>
> Child, "Your dreams come true."
>
> "There's a rhyme my mother sang to me,
>
> Starlight, star bright,
> First star I see tonight.
> Wish I may wish I might.
> Have this wish I wish tonight."

Child, "Did you ever wish on a star?"

"I did."

Child: "Can we go wishing tomorrow night?"

"Of course."[1]

The parent responds to the child's question in two ways. First, the parent answers with facts about the meteor. Second, when the child asks if it means it's a wishing star, the parent shifts his attention from scientific knowledge to his child's sense of wonder.

Adults often feel detached from their childhood. Author Katherine May said, "I want to be enchanted again." In her book *Enchantment: Awakening Wonder in an Anxious Age* (2023), she explains,

> Enchantment is small wonder magnified through meaning [and] fascination caught in the web of fable and memory. It relies on small doses of awe ... the ability to sense magic in the everyday, to channel it through our minds and bodies, to be sustained by it.
>
> (9)

The author recalls that enchantment came to her in childhood as deep engagements with the world around her. However, she laments that the pressures of growing up suppressed the way she experienced enchantment. "I thought it was what I had to do in order to grow up. It took years of work, years of carefully forgetting. I never realized what I was losing" (13).

As parents, we hope to provide our children with that which we, as children, feel we missed. Similarly, Katherine May set out to immerse her young son in the wonders of nature as they explored a woodland forest. She pointed to and named the budding trees, indicated traces of squirrels, and spaces where small animals hibernate—all to no avail. Her young son was not interested. She continued their forays through forest and oceanside and to all places the mother wanted her young son to experience and savor into his adulthood. "I want my son to inhabit deep terrains as his birthright ... to revel in the bounty of these shared spaces" (35).

"After a while," May writes, "I stopped trying to teach and [tried] to share my perceptions instead." As time and experience pass between mother and child, she notices his silence. Unable to resist the urge to know, she asks, "Is it nice there, in your head?" After a pause, her son turns slowly, "Sometimes I feel like my mind is growing branches." "Yes,! I say, delighted at this point of contact. "Yes! I know that feeling exactly." Her son replies, "And every time you talk to me, you cut one of them off" (38). Abrupt, yet, for his mother, an awakening. When we think we know our children, they surprise us. What are we to do? Listen.

As the title indicates, Alison Gopnik's *The Gardener and the Carpenter* (2016) presents the gardener and carpenter as metaphors for different parenting models. You may have guessed that Gopnik believes in Friedrich Frobel's Kindergarten gardener approach, where children play, sing, draw, and socialize. "Caring for children is like tending a garden, and being a parent is like being a gardener" (18). Moreover, she suggested that the carpenter parenting model involves working with materials you are given so that you know how they influence how you will proceed and what you will do. Accordingly, "your job is to shape that material into a final product that will fit the scheme you had in mind. And you can assess how good a job you've done by looking at the finished product." Gopnik adds, "Messiness and variability are the carpenter's enemies; precision and control are her allies" (18).

In contrast, the gardener parenting model begins with creating a nurturing and protected environment. The gardener prepares rich, fertile soil and the right amount of sunlight and water to support the flourishing young sprouts and shoots. Proper preparation and tending allow plants to grow independently according to Mother Nature's design. William Crain (2004), in *Reclaiming Childhood*, described the garden metaphor to child-centered parenting, "Similarly, we as parents can create conditions and opportunities for the child's growth, but we must trust the child to do her growing; and allow her to make her discoveries" (174). The good gardener knows that predetermined plans regularly require on-site adjustments due to differences in the youngling's strength, vigor, and beauty. *Warmth is a vital element for the growing plant and for the soul of the child*, Carl Jung.

Additionally, Gopnik writes,

> So our job as parents is not to make a particular kind of child. Instead, our job is to provide a protected environment of love, safety, and stability where children of many unpredictable kinds can flourish. Our job is not to shape our children's minds; it is to let those minds explore all the possibilities that the world allows. Our job is not to tell children how to play; it's to give them toys.

Furthermore, she wrote, "We can't make children learn, but we can let them learn."

Attachment theory, developed by John Bowlby and Mary Ainsworth, posits that the affectional bond between mother and infant is an intrinsic human need. Numerous theorists, including Daniel Stern (1985), Colin Trevarthen (2009), Sophie Alcock (2013), and others, have expanded the importance of early bonding. The parent–child attachment that begins in infancy with reciprocal touch, sound, and sight is a sacred bond. It sustains the child's sense of belonging, well-being, and trust for now and in the future.

Ellen Handler Spitz (1999) said the most important feature of parenting is enjoying your children. "Delight in them, rejoice with them, have good times together, treasure the days of your life that are spent in their company" (xv). She wrote:

> If I close my eyes and concentrate, I can even now hear my mother's voice as she read to me each evening when I was a child—both picture books and poetry. I remember the cadences and inflections, the lilt and verve of her special reading voice. Nuanced and expressive, it pronounced each word slowly and distinctly and lingered lovingly over syllables or phrases. Not at all like her normal "hurry up" voice, this one had the capacity to transport to faraway places and times [...] Best of all, it embraced me with an auditory ambience of coziness and warmth.
>
> (1)

Loving kindness between parent and child comes from being together in ways of closeness that honor children. Not the "hurry up" of everyday demands of the clock, but child-time. Time made for wonder, dreaming, and make-believe. Child time is for spontaneous play, open-ended adventures in the natural world, reading and being read to, singing together, and sharing artworks, including the many ways unique to your child and culture.

Sharing a child's enchanted world unfolds our past and present of wonder and awe. In a beautiful picture book, *When I Was a Child*, Andy Stanton and David Litchfield (2018) reveal the special bonds between a grandmother and child as they share magic, joy, and love in the present world and the past:

> *There is magic in everything.*
> *The world is a spinning star,*
> *No matter how old you are.*
>
> *Take my hand and follow me.*

Note

1 Danette Littleton.

References

Alcock, Sophie. Toddlers' Complex Communication: Playfulness from a Secure Base, *Contemporary Issues in Early Childhood*. 14 (2), 2013, 179–190.

Crain, William. *Reclaiming Childhood: Letting Children Be Children in Our Achievement Oriented Society*. Macmillan, 2004.

Gopnik, Alison. *The Gardner and the Carpenter: What the New Science of Child Development Tells Us About the Relationship Between Parents and Children*. Macmillan, 2016.

May, Katherine. *Enchantment: Awakening Wonder in an Anxious Age*. Penguin, 2023.

Spitz, Ellen Handler. *Inside Picture Books*. Yale University Press, 1999.

Stanton, Andy, and David Litchfield. *When I Was a Child*. Hachette, 2018. https://youtube/86QESyf5e0g?si=VRQUDNtfqJp1F_YP

Stern, David. *The Interpersonal World of the Infant: A View from Psychoanalysis and Developmental Psychology*. New York, 1985.

Trevarthen, Colin. The Intersubjective Psychobiology of Human Meaning, *Psychoanalytic Dialogues*, 19 (5), 507–518, 2009.

2

The Spiritual Child

Danette Littleton

The child's spirituality begins at birth. She carries a genetic bounty from generations of human development—she is baptized in stardust. Newly formed, she emerges into a new world seeking attachment and longing to belong. Her desire to connect assures her physical, psychological, and spiritual survival. Along the journey, her well-being relies on how favorably we respond to her physical care of health and safety, psychological care of attention and love, and spiritual care with sensitivity to wonder and awe.

At the first cry and cuddle, she grasps the finger of a loving mother. The palmar reflex appears at birth whenever someone's finger or a small object is placed in an infant's palm. This neonatal response creates interactions and bonding between infants, mothers, and fathers, to the delight of siblings. "She's got my finger!" Before language emerges, our baby girl coos, laughs, and chortles. In an essay, "On Laughing, Notes on the Funniest Sound There Is," Patrick Madden shares this anecdote:

> My three-month-old daughter is just beginning to laugh. She is not ticklish; she is not mimicking us. As far as I can tell, she is just delighted by the world. She sees a funny face, sees her brother in a giant witch's hat, sees me with

my eyeglasses upside down, sees her mother dancing to funky music from a commercial, and she laughs.

(2016, 19)

Where did this sense of funniness come from in a baby so soon born? Madden suggests that God has a sense of humor, citing this statement written in a third-century B.C. Egyptian papyrus: "When [God] burst out laughing, there was light. ... The waters were born when he burst out laughing the second time; at the seventh burst of laughter, the soul was born." Madden recalled God's unique sense of humor in Genesis 17:15–17.

> [15] *God also said to Abraham, "As for Sarai your wife, you are no longer to call her Sarai; her name will be Sarah.* [16] *I will bless her and will surely give you a son by her. I will bless her so that she will be the mother of nations; kings of peoples will come from her."*
> [17] *Abraham fell facedown; he laughed…*

What a concept! God and little children share a sense of humor. Isn't the laughter of babies and young children the most delightful sound in the world? Those belly-jiggling, head-tossed-back, spontaneous, and unrestrained squeals of pure joy are contagious to everyone around them, even God. Imagine a playful God of make-believe, imagination, and creativity who loves play, fun, and games. Children write to God as a personal friend in this collection of *Children's Letters to God* (1991). Their letters of innocence are charming, amusing, and yet wise.

> *Dear God, I bet it is very hard for you to love all of everybody in the whole world. There are only 4 people in our family, and I can never do it. Nan*
>
> *Dear God, It rained for are [our] whole vacation and is my father mad! He said some things about you that people are not supposed to say, but I hope you will not hurt him anyway. Your friend, But I am not going to tell you who I am.*
>
> *Dear God, If you watch in church on Sunday, I will show you my new shoes. Mickey D*

Dear God, I want to be just like you when I am your age. O.K?
Tom

Dear God, I don't ever feel alone since I found out about you. Nora

Comments such as these show that children think of God in their image within a personal world of faith, hope, and kindness. Their inner life manifests daily and everywhere: at play, in nature, in secret, and silence. Open-mindedness, intuitiveness, and spontaneity characterize children's capacity to wonder without a factual explanation. Van Manen (1996) suggested that reliance on factual information is the greatest hindrance to the phenomenon of wonder, thereby limiting our complete understanding of meaning (251).

Joseph Campbell (Campbell and Moyers 2011), eminent mythographer and author of *The Power of Myth* and *The Hero's Journey*, said, "Inner world experience is not quantifiable, not supernatural, but real experience." Thomas Merton, an American Trappist monk, theologian, mystic, and prolific writer on spirituality and social justice, said, "Children are naturally hopeful. This may have something to do with their sensitivity to the marvel of life. They do not calculate or plan. They prefer to be surprised" (45).

Play is the spiritual language of children, but some adults need to remember how to speak it. Adults have much to learn from children's playful attitudes toward life. Brian Edgar wrote in *The God Who Plays* (2017) that, according to Jesus of Nazareth, people should learn from little children "and that a spirituality of play is to be preferred to one of self-denial" (15). Here, Jesus turned the wisdom of the learned and the social order upside down.

Now, they were bringing even infants to him so that he might touch them. When the disciples saw this, they rebuked them. But Jesus called them to him, saying, "Let the children come to me and do not hinder them, for to such belongs the kingdom of God. Truly, I say to you, whoever does not receive the kingdom of God like a child shall not enter it."

Luke 18:15–17 ESV

Brian Edgar describes a pathway to God as one of joy instead of self-sacrifice: "This approach to the spiritual life stresses the beauty and goodness of God's creation and complete engagement with the world. It involves an appreciation of art, an attitude of playfulness, and an outlook permeated with deep joy" (16).

Play occurs on hallowed ground—a sacred space where invented worlds are real. In an episode of free play, three four-year-old girls pretend that a dangerous stranger suddenly appears. Throughout the spontaneous interactions, each child contributes to the development of the drama, similar to actors performing improvisations live and on-stage. They begin without prompts or pre-arranged discussions. Each player builds on the others' ideas. Suddenly, Holly blurts out:

Holly: *Pretend one day there was a robber.*
Jenny: *Yeah. Pretend one day there was a robber and he came in and I put some magic on the floor, and he slipped.*
Margaret: *Pretend you're the robber.*
Holly: *NO!*
Margaret: *Pretend I hear a thump, and it woke you up. Now, here's the thump.* (She makes a loud stomping sound.)

Shocked, the children realize their money is gone. They take turns looking and discover it hidden under the couch. At their triumph over the robber, Jenny declares with authority, *"They are stupid!"* Holly replies with disgust. *"Dumb-dumbs!"*

In a different twenty-minute dramatic episode, Belinda, Tara, and Holly initiated themes of homelessness, crime, and drugs as though they were adult characters in a scripted play. Their improvisations were emotionally charged in speech and gesture, resulting in a well-constructed drama with an imaginative *denouement*. A playroom is the setting for house play. Abruptly, Belinda sets the scene:

Belinda: *These people are keeping us here.*
Tara: *We should leave. How long do we have to stay here?*
Holly: *I don't know.*

Belinda:	*Hey, look! Shoes around! Pencils around! Papers around! It's a junky house.*
Holly:	*This looks like a garage sale.*
Belinda:	*This is an old junkyard. And I can't do anything about it. (Children begin to argue about what to do.)*
Holly:	*No! All we need is a new house and a garage sale!*
Belinda:	*All we need to do is clean up this JUNK HOUSE! (Belinda starts throwing things about.)*
Holly:	*No! you can't throw that out because the policeman will catch you ... and catch you ... and catch you!*
Belinda:	*The policemen around here can't shoot! They have no guns! Broken windows! And signs in the windows ... and robbers, and people in the streets getting killed ... and dirty people.*
Holly:	*And people giving candy with cocaine in it! And they come to our door and said, "Who wants candy?" And it had cocaine in it. And what do you want for BAD COCAINE?*
Belinda:	*And dirty people, and dirty containers ... and dying people and robbers. And trash everywhere!*
Holly:	*Yes.*
Belinda:	*And dirty flowers.*
Holly:	*NO dirty flowers.*
Tara:	*I can't stand it here.*
Belinda:	*I guess we'll have to move.*
Tara:	*Me too ... a different world.*
Belinda:	*It's just a dirty old junkyard world, and I don't know why we have to live here anyway.*
Holly:	*Go to Hawaii!*
Belinda:	*That's a nice place. Let's go to Hawaii!*
Holly:	*Let's get our clothes and go to Hawaii! I'll pack up first.*
Tara:	*Let's go!*

The house-play episode ends with the girls trying on play clothes and chatting about dresses and shoes. The junkyard world is not mentioned again. As in many other play episodes in this study, young children demonstrate their creativity and the power of imagination through play's influence on and advancement of cognitive and social development (Littleton, 1991).

This three-month study was designed to discover the influence of free-play settings on children's play behaviors. The results demonstrated that free play settings powerfully influence young children's advancement of cognitive, social, and musical development (Littleton, 1991).

Dutch historian Johann Huizinga, in his seminal work, *Homo Ludens, A Study of the Play-Element in Culture*, wrote, "Just as there is no formal difference between play and ritual, so the 'consecrated spot' cannot be formally distinguished from the playground. [...] All are temporary worlds within the ordinary world, dedicated to the performance of an act apart" (1938/1950).

Notably, various play spaces offer children differing learning experiences. Consider the free play of young children in classrooms, on the playground, and in nature's wild places. Structured only by the ecology of the setting, free play allows children to seek and solve problems independently, learn how to socialize with other children, see their points of view, modulate emotions, and negotiate disagreements.

In *Outdoor Play: Teaching Strategies with Young Children* (2001), author-ethnographer Jane P. Perry studies young children's play outdoors and the supportive roles of teachers. The present case study includes videotape observations of children in the play yard, audiotape reviews of the videotapes by two teachers involved in the study, and Perry's field notes. Like children's free play in classroom settings, Perry found recurring make-believe play themes and actions in outdoor settings. "The flexibility of play cues allows for a distinct expression and manifestation of the world of young children from their own cultural play perspective" (2). "Ecology of play" defines a play space with play materials and players where children often communicate "ecological cues" without spoken words.

What if children could design their outdoor play environments? White and Stoecklin suggest they would create play spaces entirely unlike those made for them by adults. Research on children's preferences shows that "Outdoor spaces designed by children would not only be fully naturalized with plants, trees, flowers, dirt, sand, mud, animals and insects but also would be rich with a wider variety of play opportunities" (1998, 1).

Numerous studies by Charles Lewis (1996), Anita Barrows (1995), Ruth Wilson (1997), Robin Moore (1997), and others have shown that children's experiences in wilderness and natural areas engender positive feelings of well-being and connection with nature. Edith Cobb (1977) demonstrated that children's sense of wonder, engendered by playing freely in nature, is foundational to creative learning.

Researchers and caregivers agree that children's outdoor play differs from indoor play.

For example, exceptional differences in sensory experiences, greater freedom for physical and noisy activities, opportunities to interact with the environment, exploring and utilizing loose parts, and generally abandoning indoor rules of disorder and making a mess. Playground equipment standards and construction have improved over the years for safety and inventiveness. However, indoor play settings cannot substitute for children's freedom in wild places, magical world-building, surprise at something new at every twist and turn, and the beauty only nature can provide.

Children are worried about Mother Earth. She tells us she needs our help: "When I am in trouble, Earthlings are in trouble, too." The children's book, *Our Planet! There's No Place Like Earth* (2022), by Stacy McAnulty, magically illustrated by David Litchfield, gently warns about climate change and provides child and parent Earthlings ways to help, share stuff, buy less new stuff, and recycle.

Chapter Notes

I volunteered to teach music in a Head Start class with three-year-olds in a rural Appalachian community. In the first session, my always-successful and joyful teaching was failing. The children would not look at me. I introduced a song and offered the children small percussion instruments. They did not sing and refused to touch a drum or bells. "What did I do wrong?" Their teacher explained, "To them, you are a stranger. They live in a small, isolated community where they feel comfortable. Even adjusting to coming here was difficult."

Before the next session, I wondered," How can I gain their trust?" Quietly and silently, I entered the play area. I brought a Raggedy Ann doll about the size of a toddler and placed the doll in my lap, her face covering mine, and began to sing. As I sang, I moved Raggedy Ann's arms and legs to the tempo, rhythm, and phrase structures. She was a great success in engaging and holding the children's interest and feeling of comfort. They enjoyed playing the small percussion instruments, puppets, picture books, and all the music play materials I brought to them.

If you have taught young children, you know that time-allotted scheduling does not suit them. Instead, I created a "soft landing" instead of an abrupt stop. Informally, I chatted with the children and asked, "Would you like to play with this?" Timidly, at first, but over the year I met with them, they freely played with instruments, puppets, and songbooks, spontaneously exploring and making music. Findings about music practices in preschool and early childhood classes denied free play with music, "They do not know how to play," or they might damage the instruments."

On the contrary, my videotape documentation showed young children engaged in self-initiated, spontaneous, imaginative music playing without adult intervention. Interest in how children play with music led me to the first significant study of children's free play with music: the seminal Pillsbury Studies by Moorhead and Pond (1941).

Teaching and learning experiences with one group of three-year-old children from the hills of east Tennessee led me to a lifetime of teaching, observing, and studying young children's free play with music.

References

Barrows, Anita. "The Ecopsychology of Child Development," *Ecopsychology*, edited by Rozak, Gomes, & Tanner, Sierra Club Books, 1995.

Campbell, Joseph, and Bill Moyers. *The Power of Myth*. Anchor, 2011.

Cobb, Edith. *The Ecology of Imagination in Childhood*. Columbia University Press, 1977.

Edgar, Brian. *The God Who Plays: A Playful Approach to Theology and Spirituality*. Stock Publishers, 2017.

Hample, Stuart, and Eric Marshall. *Children's Letters to God*. Workman, 1991.

Huizinga, Johan. *Homo Ludens: A Study of the Play-Element in Culture*. Routledge, 1950.

Lewis, Charles A. *Green Nature, Human Nature: The Meaning of Plants in Our Lives*. University of Illinois Press, 1996.

Littleton, Danette. *Influence of Play Settings on Preschool Children's Music and Play Behaviors*. University of Texas at Austin, 1991.

Madden, Patrick. "On Laughing: Notes of the Funniest Sound There Is" in Doyle, Brianed, *A Sense of Wonder: The World's Best Writers on the Sacred, the Profane, and the Ordinary*. Orbis, 2016.

McAnulty, Stacy and David Litchfield. *Our Planet! There's No Place Like Earth*. Henry Holt and Company, 2022.

Moorhead, Gladys, and Donald Pond. *Music of Young Children*. The Pillsbury Foundation for the Advancement of Music Education, 1941.

Moore, Robin C., and Herb H. Hong. *Natural Learning: Creating Environments for Rediscovering Nature's Way of Teaching*. MIG Communications, 1997.

Perry, Jane P. *Outdoor Play: Teaching Strategies with Young Children*. Teachers College Press, 2001.

Van Manen, Max, and Bas Levering. *Childhood Secrets: Intimacy, Privacy, and the Self Reconsidered*. Teachers College Press, 1996.

White, Randy and Vicki Stoecklin. "Children's Outdoor Play & Learning Environments: Returning to Nature." *Early Childhood News*. March–April 1998 issue.

Wilson, Ruth A. "The Wonders of Nature - Honoring Children's Ways of Knowing," *Early Childhood News*. March–April 1997.

3

The Natural Child

Danette Littleton

Children, real and imaginary, relish independence. They trust their senses, feelings, intuition, and imagination more than others. Consider Huckleberry Finn, a child of nature by necessity and choice. Huck, motherless with a no-good father, sets off to live by his wits in the woods and river around him. William Crain (2004) quotes Mark Twain's (2007) introduction to Huck in *The Adventures of Tom Sawyer*:

> Huckleberry came and went of his own free will. He slept on doorsteps in fine weather and empty hogsheads [barrels] in wet; he did not have to go to school or church, call any being master, or obey anybody; he could go fishing or swimming when or where he chose. In a word, everything that goes to make life precious, that boy had.
>
> (189)

Obviously, Huck's lifestyle is impossible and dangerous for children of today, but perhaps our children need a sense of belonging to the natural world such as Huck's: "He listens to the moods and messages of the wind; he senses the friendliness of squirrels; he feels the joy of the birds at daybreak and plants along the river" (198). Huck feels the stillness of the river and the stillness in him, "lazying around [on his raft] and listening to the stillness."

Wild Child is a symbolic picture book that tells what happens when a fearless and unencumbered child who thrives in the natural world becomes the "very, very last child left in the wild." Long out of print, *Wild Child* was written in charming rhythmic verse by Jeanne Willis and illustrated by Lorna Freytag (2012). Unable to gain copyright permission to quote the actual book, I offer my summary of *Wild Child*.

> *The wild child calls the sun and wind and thunderous storms Father.*
> *Moon and sea and stars and earth, she calls Mother.*
> *Animals, large and small, are her brothers and sisters.*
> *She lives wherever she wishes and finds food and water to her taste.*

All is peaceful until the grown-ups come looking for the wild children. You know what happens next: They are caught! The last child explains why there are no feral children left today. The adults have taken away all their wildness, wisdom, and habitats.

> *They made them do sums and wear sensible shoes.*
> *They put them to bed at the wrong times of the day.*
> *They made them sit still when they wanted to play.*
> *They made them say pardon and please.*

The stories of Huck and the Wild Child are fiction; do not try to copy their lifestyles with your children. However, each story has meaning for how we approach caring for and teaching children. Technologies permeate the lives of children today; there is no going back, nor would we wish it so. Yet, too many children live indoor lives with less free time and more structured time, organized activities, play dates, and summer camps. So, if you know any children who are too wild or tame, take them to forests, mountains, rivers, and the seaside and set them free.

Richard Louv (2008) calls for a nature–child reunion in *The Last Child in the Woods: Saving Our Children from Nature-*

Deficit Disorder. Passionate about the meaning of children's deep engagement in nature and dedicated to authentic research, Louv initiated an international movement through his books and as co-founder of the non-profit Children & Nature Network. Louv explains how today's children are bereft of the benefits of playing in and experiencing the world of nature and why it matters to children at any age. Throughout his book, he characterizes a new relationship between child and nature.

In "Multiple Intelligences after Twenty Years," Howard Gardner, a paper presented at the American Educational Research Association in Chicago in 2003, added an eighth intelligence: the naturalist. Citing Charles Darwin, John Muir, and Rachel Carson, Garner explained:

> The core of the naturalist intelligence is the human ability to recognize plants, animals, and other parts of the natural environment, like clouds or rocks. All of us can do this; some kids (experts on dinosaurs) and many adults (hunters, botanists, anatomists) excel at this pursuit. While the ability doubtless evolved to deal with natural kinds of elements. I believe that it has been hijacked to deal with the world of man-made objects. We are good at distinguishing among cars, sneakers, and jewelry, for example, because our ancestors needed to be able to recognize carnivorous animals, poisonous snakes, and flavorful mushrooms.
>
> (quoted in Louv, 2008, 72)

Larry Prochner, a professor of early childhood education at the University of Alberta in Edmonton, studies children's education in nature. His article "Our Proud Heritage: Take it Outside: A History of Nature-Based Education" (2021) reviews the past 200 years of ideas and practices in nature-based education for young children. He defines this concept as children's active learning in the natural world, whether in a neighborhood park or forest. Historically, viewpoints and practices have varied; consider the nature study movement in the United States, 1890–1920. "Educators, psychologists, and biologists worried that children's development was being harmed by life in an industrial society, a 'book-based' school curriculum, and teacher-centered methods" (6). Nature-based education supplanted the former method to correct this harm by emphasizing children's observation and experience in the "natural and human-centered worlds."

Nature-based learning yields developmental value to children's health, principles of right and wrong, creativity, imagination, and spirituality. Edith Cobb, in *The Ecology of Imagination in Childhood* (1977), wrote: "The child's ecological sense of continuity with nature is not what is generally known as mystical. It is, I believe, basically aesthetic and infused with joy in the power to know and to be" (23).

Each child grows and develops according to an inner biological and genetic determination guided by nature and children's instincts, curiosity, and the urgency to learn. Author Ellen Handler Spitz, *Inside Picture Books* (1999), advised that while parenting is never simple, it is particularly complex and challenging in times like ours. "If asked what I consider to be the most important feature of parenting, I would say without hesitation ... simply enjoyment" (xv). Our greatest joy comes as a conduit for children's discoveries, especially when we find the right balance between leading and following. Children never exhaust their energy for life and the things they love-*Ro Take my hand and follow me*.

Many poets and artists, explorers, and scientists recall their early years as the cradle of a lifetime of discovery and accomplishment. A stuffed toy chimpanzee, "Jubilee," led Jane Goodall to lifetime studies of chimpanzees in the wild. Orville and Wilbur Wright's father gave his young boys a 1-foot-long aerodynamic toy helicopter to play with. When it finally broke, the boys built another one. John Muir, a naturalist, explored the meadows, wooded hills, and seacoast of his birthplace in Scotland. In boyhood, he loved reading adventure stories. Despite Helen Keller's childhood disabilities, she became world-famous as an author and speaker. She championed the rights of people with disabilities and the poor. She was a lifelong suffragette and Christian socialist.

Harold Robles (2017), author, and founder of the Albert Schweitzer Institute for the Humanities, said that from the age of eight, he followed the humanitarian life of Albert Schweitzer. In *Reverence for Life: The Words of Albert Schweitzer*, he wrote,

> By his example and devoted service to suffering humanity, Dr. Schweitzer tested the [consciousness] of all people. And he gave the world a philosophy, one by which he lived his life and which he felt expressed the hope and and promise of civilization. He called it 'Ehrfurcht vor den Leben,' Reverence for Life.
>
> (xvii)

Finally, this is a true-life story about imagination, wisdom, and resilience: children making a way out of no way. The story (Friedland & Mandela 2003) is set in Qunu, a village in South Africa where Nelson Mandela was born and played as a boy. Rural life was basic and plain, with beehive-shaped mud-walled houses and farm animals nearby. When circumstances prevented Shaka and Nandi, his little sister, from attending school, they had to stay home. Father had a new job located too far away for him to walk his children to school, and it was too dangerous for them to walk alone. Shaka and Nandi decided they *must* find a way to return to school. They thought about selling things at the market to buy a bus. Then, they wondered if a bus could be built out of throw-away materials. Nothing worked, but they did not give up. Shaka had an idea. He told his mother, "We found another way. We'll walk together like a moving bus, but there's no real bus! It's just us. With enough of us, we can look after each other—a walking school bus."

Many children, such as Shaka and Nandi, walk over two hours to school in countries like South Africa. Along the way, they hold hands, sing songs, and pick fruit for lunch. These children trust their intuition and imagination and are courageous and undaunted, characteristics of the natural child.

References

Cobb, Edith. *The Ecology of Imagination in Childhood.* Columbia University Press, 1977.

Crain, William. *Reclaiming Childhood: Letting Children Be Children in Our Achievement Oriented Society.* Macmillan, 2004.

Friedland, Aaron, and Ndileka Mandela. *The Walking School Bus.* Greystone Books, 2003.

Louv, Richard. *Last Child in the Woods: Saving Our Children from Nature-Deficit Disorder.* Algonquin Books of Chapel Hill, 2008.

Prochner, Larry. "Our Proud Heritage. Take It Outside: A History of Nature-Based Educations," *Young Children*, Fall, 2021.

Robles, Harold E. (Ed.). *Reverence for Life: The Words of Albert Sweitzer.* Maurice Bassett, 1993/2017.

Spitz, Ellen Handler. *Inside Picture Books.* Yale University Press, 1999.

Twain, Mark. *The Adventures of Tom Sawyer.* Oxford University Press, 2007.

Willis, Jeanne. *Wild Child.* Walker Books, 2012.

4
The Mystical Child

Danette Littleton

Young children, like mystics, accept the seen and unseen, named and unnamed, and known and unknown in the living world. These early sojourners trust their insights, intuition, and purity of perception instead of logical reasoning. Marsha Sinetar, in *Spiritual Intelligence* (2000), suggests that children express an early awakening of themselves and are faithful to an inner guide. "That awakening," she concluded, "approaches the illumination long held by the mystical tradition" (2). To consider how this awakening in children might hold qualities of mysticism, we looked at the lives of mystics and their insights.

In *The Mystic Heart* (2001), Wayne Teasdale wrote that the mystical tradition underpins all genuine faith. [It] "is the living source of religion itself. It is the attempt to possess the inner reality of the spiritual life, with its mystical, or direct, access to the divine" (11). Before the emergence of world religions, mysticism thrived for thousands of years. It enriched expressions of faith by ancient and contemporary mystics, such as, but not limited to, Hildegard of Bingen, Moses Maimonides, St. Francis of Assisi, Mother Julian of Norwich, *The Cloud of Unknowing*, Theresa of Avila, Mahatma Gandhi, Evelyn Underhill, Thomas Merton, Martin Buber, Mother Theresa, Dali Lama, and poets such as Rumi, Hafiz, Tagore, William Wordsworth, William Blake, Henry David Thoreau, and many others. There are common elements and characteristics among mystics across traditions, time, and place. Presented here are a few of the many who shaped religious faith.

Moses Maimonides (1135–1204), a rabbi, physician, and Torah scholar, was born in Spain and lived in Egypt and Morocco. He was considered one of Jewish history's most essential and prolific philosophers. His body of work is studied worldwide today.

> *There is no difference between the pain of humans and the pain of other living beings since the love and tenderness of the mother for the young are not produced by reasoning but by feeling, and this faculty exists not only in humans but in most living beings.*

In *The Sacred Code: The Mysterious Formula That Rules Art, Nature, and Science* (2008) Priya Hemenway writes:

> What the Greeks knew intuitively about music was naturally reflected in the experience of *Logos*; for music *is* harmony. Harmony *is* music: It is the most natural expression of the mathematical laws the Pythagoreans discovered, and their mystical teachings attributed great significance to it.
>
> There is a theory that early Christian mystics, when they referred to *Logos* or "the Word" were referring to music. We hear in the New Testament of the Bible that "In the beginning was the Word and the Word was with God, and the Word was God." There are many ways to understand this beautiful statement. It is interesting to note that where we now read "Word" the Greek text has *Logos*.
>
> (181)

Moreover, the Indian mystic Osho (1931–1990) expressed thoughts on the inner music of the soul, heart, and mind. "… all your layers of being are full of it. Once known, not only do you hear it inside of you, but it is outside, too. In the song of birds, you hear it, and in the winds passing through the trees you hear it, and in the waves striking on the rocks you hear it. In sound you hear it, in silence, you hear it.

> The greatest music in the world is nothing but an echo of the inner music.
>
> (183)

Hildegarde of Bingen (1098–1115), a German abbess, mystic, and visionary of theology, and musician, composed over seventy liturgical songs, canticles, and Psalms settings, three books about her visions, spiritual life, treatises on healing and health, and numerous correspondences with heads of Church and State who sought her advice. In *The Journal of Hildegard of Bingen: Inspired by a Year in the Life of the Twelfth Century Mystic* (1993), Barbara Lachman transcribed the following journal passage December 1, 1151, The First Sunday in Advent:

> *The last vision was more like a visitation; it was so fleeting, simple, direct, and wordless in the few seconds I allowed for contemplation. Outside the casement, I saw the broad sycamore tree once again shorn of its leaves, its branches grappling with the winter sky, its base solidly in the earth. Suddenly, the tree began physically to move in the quiet midday. Its motion seems such that I and everything I know or could imagine were present in that tree and shared the same fluid, energetic breathing. The privileged glimpse was gone in a moment, though I have no doubt the joyous movement continues still.*

St. Francis of Assisi (1181–1226) eschewed a life of privilege and wealth for one of selflessness and poverty as a beggar and itinerant preacher. Considered by some to be Italy's first poet, he left numerous written rules and admonitions, prayers, songs, and letters. In *The Song of Brother Sun and All His Creatures*, St. Francis of Assisi (1964) wrote:

> *Praise to thee, My Lord, for all thy creatures,*
> *Above all, Brother Sun*
> *Who brings us the day and lends us his light.*

St. Francis expressed his precept of faith in *The Counsels of the Holy Father Saint Francis, Admonition 27*:

Where there is charity and wisdom, there is neither fear nor ignorance.

Where there is patience and humility, there is neither anger nor vexation.

Where there is poverty and joy, there is neither greed nor avarice.

Where there is peace and meditation, there is neither anxiety nor doubt.

Julian (Juliana) of Norwich (1343–after 1416), mystic anchoress and theologian, wrote that while recovering from a severe illness, she received visions from God that transformed her secular life into a contemplative one. She withdrew from society for permanent seclusion in a singular cell. Juliana's theological writings are the earliest surviving in English by a woman and the only works by an anchorite, a religious recluse who lives in permanent meditative seclusion. In the introduction to *Revelations of Divine Love*, Juliana wrote of the first revelation, "in which all the revelations which follow are founded and connected" (*Julian of Norwich: Showings*, 1998, 26). Throughout her writings, she maintains the monastic tradition "that every human happiness is a participation in divine beatitude…" (62). Continuing, this is her definition:

Prayer is a right understanding of that fullness of joy which is to come, with true longing and trust. The savouring or seeing of our bliss, to which we are ordained by nature makes us to long; true understanding and love, with a sweet recollection in our savour, by grace makes us to trust.

(62)

Even before writing was invented, indigenous people gave evidence of their mystical beliefs about the natural world – the sun and moon, the earth, human origins, and animal spirits. In their search for spiritual meaning, First Peoples expressed their discoveries through stories, rituals, drawings, structures, chants, songs, and dances.

"In our old religion, we believed that the Great Spirit who made all things is in everything, and with every breath of air, we drew in the life of the Great Spirit" in *The Indians' Book*, 1923/1968, as told by Big Thunder of the Wabanakis Tribe (4).

From Black Elk (1863–1950):

Everything an Indian does is in a circle, and that is because the power of the world always works in circles, and everything tries to be round. In the old days, when we were a strong and happy people, all our power came to us from the sacred hoop of the nation, and so as long as the hoop was unbroken, the people flourished.
(Bartlett's Familiar Quotations, 1992, 587)

In the Trail of the Wind: Indian Poems and Ritual Orations, John Bierhorst (1971) collected and edited songs, chants, prayers, and speeches in the oral literature from First Nations of North America. Bierhorst explained that long before the arrival and contact with Europeans, "Indian literature was passed down through the aid of pictographs (Chippewa) mnemonic beads (Iroquois) or books elaborated painted with glyphs (Maya)" (30). Bierhorst said that Indian poetry came down primarily as song-texts but also as prayers, incantations, and passages from myths and legends. "All of these were transmitted carefully from generation to generation" (2). A song-text from the Navajo (19):

It was the wind that gave them life.

It is the wind that comes out of our mouths now that gives us life.

When this ceases to blow, we die.

In the skin at the tips of our fingers, we see the trail of the wind.

It shows us where the wind blew when our ancestors were created.

To clarify, spirituality and mysticism are related but not the same. All mystics are spiritual, but not all those who engage in spirituality, sacred or secular, are mystics. In our study of spirituality, we discovered distinctions were rarely made between spirituality and mysticism; often, the terms were interchangeable. To illustrate, Philip Sheldrake (2007) explored spirituality, and Evelyn Underhill in *Mysticism* (1955) wrote of spirituality that humans are vision-makers, not merely tool-makers, and that humans are seekers of life's deeper meaning. Robert Coles (1991) explored children's spirituality through ways of knowing, experiencing, and expressing personal thoughts. Daniel Hay and Rebecca Nye (1998/2006) concluded that exploring wonder, awe, and imagination reveals children's spirituality. Tobin Hart (2010) identified children's mystical capacities as evidenced by wisdom, wonder, and seeing the invisible. Marsha Sinetar (2000) introduced children's spiritual intelligence as an early awakening to their inner lives and compared it to the mystical tradition.

The qualitative differences between spirituality and mysticism are meaningful but rarely defined, especially concerning children. With Wayne Teasdale (2001), we profess that "children are born with a simplicity of heart. It is a natural simplicity or purity inherent in children" (151). Children demonstrate an immediate heightened awareness of the mystical. *Hearing* children means recognizing children's outward symbols and signs of their inner world, that is, a mystical way of knowing.

When I Was a Child, by Andy Stanton and David Litchfield (2018)

There are faces in the raindrops,
the world is a diamond string.
There is wonder in everything.

There are heartbeats in the mountains,
The world is a blue guitar ...
The world is a spinning star ...
... no matter how old you are.

In later chapters, we will present narratives of children's mystical states of being, giving evidence of and affirming their inner world of illumination.

References

Bierhorst, John. *In the Trail of the Wind: American Indian Poems and Ritual Orations*. Farrar Straus Giroux, 1971.

Coles, Robert. *The Spiritual Life of Children*. Houghton Mifflin, 1991.

Francis, Saint. *The Writings of Saint Francis of Assisi*. Franciscan Herald Press, 1964.

Hay, Daniel, and Rebecca Nye. *The Spirit of the Child*. Jessica Kingsley Publishers, 2006.

Hemenway, Priya. *The Secret Code: The Mysterious Formula That Rules Art, Nature, and Science*. Evergreen, 2008.

Julian of Norwich. *Revelations of Divine Love*. Penguin UK, 1998.

Lachman, Barbara. *The Journal of Hildegard of Bingen: Inspired by a Year in the Life of the Twelfth Century Mystic*. Bell Tower, 1993.

Sheldrake, Philip. *A Brief History of Spirituality*. John Wiley and Sons, 2007.

Sinetar, Marsha. *Spiritual Intelligence: What We Can Learn from the Early Awakening Child*. Orbis Books, 2000.

Stanton, Andy, and David Litchfield. *When I Was a Child*. Hodder's Children's Books, 2018.

Teasdale, Wayne. *The Mystic Heart: Discovering a Universal Spirituality in the World's Religions*. New World Library, 2001.

Underhill, Evelyn. *Mysticism: A Study in the Nature and Development of Man's Spiritual Consciousness*. Meridian Books, 1955.

5

Framing Portraits

Danette Littleton and Meryl Sole

"The quieter we become, the more we can hear," said Rumi, a 12th-century Persian mystic. Quiet listening is the key to accessing children's mystical insights—in contrast, interviews, questioning, and commenting as research strategies trespass on children's inner thoughts. Elliot Eisner, leading scholar and educator of arts in education, questioned traditional assumptions that research should only be measurable and quantifiable. Eisner redefined the field of inquiry by demonstrating the value of descriptive, narrative work to understand the meaning of experience (*Reimagining Schools: The Selected Works of Elliot Eisner* [2005]). In the article "Art in Science?," Elliot Eisner and Kimberly Powell reflect on twofold connections between art and science. They conceive of scientific research as an artistic practice where the researcher utilizes a visual arrangement of data. Through this process, patterns reveal themes and yield a multi-layered four-part *fugue* of information. The art of the research process is marked by improvisation as the work takes on form, and ideas are shaped and reshaped in harmony. "Research is performed as "artful thinking in action."

Eisner references Clifford Geertz, who said that anthropologists' most difficult challenge is the ability to research a culture and convey it in a text that convinces us of having truly been there. The renowned cultural anthropologist Geertz remade the traditional approach by borrowing from different disciplines, such as "economic development, social organization, comparative history, and cultural ecology" (xvi). His seminal work, *The Interpretation of Cultures* (1973/2000), advanced "interpretative anthropology" as a form of knowledge. Not a method, technique, or procedure; he asserts, "What defines it is the kind of intellectual effort it is: an elaborate venture in, to borrow a notion from Gilbert Ryle, 'thick description'"(6). While often attributed to Geertz, he makes clear that Ryle originated the concept of thick description.

According to Geertz, gestures, images, and objects share a semiotic importance equal to the spoken text. He writes, "The whole point of a semiotic approach to culture is to aid us in gaining access to the conceptual world in which our subjects live so that we can, in some extended sense of the term, converse with them" (27). Geertz addresses the problem of cultural theory development regarding the tension between an approach to semiotic action and satisfying technical knowledge requirements. He suggests that both, in access to the cultural world and analysis of results, are "necessarily great and essentially irremovable." [...] And that "the further theoretical development goes, the deeper the tension gets" (27).

Robert Darnton concluded in the Foreword to Geertz's *The Interpretation of Culture*, "His genius, I believe, consisted in grasping a thread in such a way as to unravel an entire pattern of culture. How he did it remains a mystery" (ix). Sara Lawrence-Lightfoot, professor of education at Harvard University, introduces portraiture as a method of qualitative research that blurs the boundaries of aesthetics and empiricism (xv) in her book *The Art and Science of Portraiture* (2002) with Jessica Hoffmann Davis, director of Arts in Education and lecturer at Harvard. In Chapter 1, Lawrence-Lightfoot cites Clifford Geertz as a point of reference for portraiture. She writes that Geertz underscores the "creative," the imaginative "tableau." He claims that anthropological writings are "fiction" (15), something made, something fashioned, and he likens his ethnographic work to the task of painting a likeness (8). Lawrence-Lightfoot explains that portraiture research aims to capture the complexities of human experience, such as the voices, visions, authority, knowledge, and wisdom of those being studied (xv). According to her, the process of portraiture in creating and documenting narratives ultimately reveals themes toward constructing a central story. In all its manifestations, storytelling requires authenticity by the researcher and for those being studied (12). This applies to children at play and artists who paint, create music, or write as they engage in or are absorbed with story-making.

In *One Writer's Beginnings* (1983), esteemed American author Eudora Welty provides compelling and profound insights into her writing process. She begins her childhood in this autobiography by writing,

> Long before I wrote stories, I listened for stories. Listening *for* them is something more acute than listening *to* them. I suppose it's an early form of participation in what goes on. Listening children know stories are *there*. When their elders sit and begin [conversing], children are just waiting and hoping for one [a story] to come out, like a mouse from its hole.
>
> (14)

As a child, Eudora relished talkers, particularly of her mother's seamstress who constantly talked to herself while sewing. Eudora said, "I dare say she *was* an author." Whether being read to or listening to elders, young Eudora said she heard stories in scenes. When she was read to and began to read to herself, she *heard* the stories line by line. The voice, she explained, was not her mother's or even her own; it was the voice of the story itself, a reader's voice. Even words had a sensory meaning for young Eudora. She richly described standing alone in her front yard on a late summer day, watching the moonrise. "For the first time, it met my eyes as a globe. The word 'moon' came into my mouth as though fed to me out of a silver spoon. It had the roundness of a Concord grape Grandpa took off his vine and gave it to me to suck out of its skin and swallow whole" (10). *Seeing* the story scenes, *hearing* the story voices, and *tasting* the words distinguish Welty's writing style. "In writing, as in life, the connections of all sorts of relationships and kinds lie in wait of discovery and give out their signals to the Geiger counter of the charged imagination, once it is drawn into the right field" (99).

While qualitative research has many iterations, processes, and applications, we propose a new system of purpose and procedures to investigate children's spontaneous experiences of spirituality. Dr. Sole's collection of vignettes with children engaging in and responding to unusual and extraordinary occurrences in various cultural settings is one source of our inquiry. No singular approach meets our research requirements; therefore, we investigated studies by an arts educator, anthropologist, sociologist, fiction writer, and Greek fables in search of guiding themes and theoretical connections. In summary, Eisner's aesthetic work on narrative themes and artistic thinking provided a vital link to anthropologist Geertz's semiotic conceptualization of culture involving gestures, images, and objects. Lawrence-Lightfoot cited Geertz as contributing to her perception of portraiture, a strategy of creating narratives through voices, visions, knowledge, and wisdom to reveal a central story. Lawrence-Lightfoot's emphasis on story-making led to Eudora Welty, who, in her autobiography, wrote that her writing style emerged in childhood and remained throughout her life. She explained that throughout the process of reading or story-writing, she *heard* stories, *saw* scenes, and *tasted* words.

Thinking about these threads and patterns, narrative themes, portraiture, and sensory recall, I remembered the myth of Ariadne's Thread, the meaning of the labyrinth, an ancient spiritual tool, and the significance of the spiritual journey. I first learned of Ariadne's Thread when I attended an opera performance of Richard Strauss's (1988) *Ariadne auf Naxo*s. My good friend Robert Dean Smith sang the tenor role of Bacchus. Attending with his wife, my childhood friend Janice Harper Smith, opera singer and coach, she introduced me to the story of Ariadne's Thread. Fascinating to learn more, I found many ancient and modern versions of the Ariadne myth that began in ancient Greece.

Charlotte Higgins, In *Red Thread: On Mazes & Labyrinths* (2018), recalled as a young child with her family visited Crete and the Bronze Age ruins of a Minoan castle in the port city of

Knossos. "I can remember the guide saying that the myth of the labyrinth started here" (9). He told the story of Minos, king of Crete, who ordered Daedalus to build a labyrinth to contain the Minotaur, the half-man, half-bull monster, terrifying everyone, especially children. Enter Theseus, king of Athens. He slays the Minotaur and, helped by Minos's daughter, Ariadne, finds his way out of the labyrinth. According to legend, Ariadne gave Theseus a ball of red thread to guide him through the twists and turns of the labyrinth, kill the Minotaur, and use the red thread to find his way back to her. Her story's ending has been retold in archeology, literature, religion, visual art, music, and film. Some versions say Theseus abandoned her, and she died on Naxos. Some say she was rescued by her true love, Bacchus.

In the classical Greek myth of The Three Fates, a thread represents time as a lifeline or means of rescue: Sleeping Beauty, Rumpelstiltskin, The Spindle, The Shuttle, and The Needle. The great-grandmother's invisible thread is beautifully woven into the story of *The Princess and the Goblin* by George MacDonald, author, and Jessie Wilcox Smith, illustrator (1911/2018).

> This fairy tale captures a glimpse of what it is like to walk a sacred oath. By following an invisible thread, we connect to the Source, to the Sacred. We can't see it, and yet some deep part of us knows it is there. This awareness gives us solace and Peace during stormy times. [...] The great-grandmother's thread is the God within, who has long been ignored and forgotten and who waits to be discovered in our own castles.
>
> (Artress, 1995/2006, 12–13)

Historical evidence shows that labyrinths and implied threads appeared thousands of years before Minos and his era. Artifacts include a bracelet found in Ukraine, dated 13,000 BCE. Stone walking labyrinths were discovered from the Paleolithic era, and rock and stone from the Neolithic epoch. Clay and bone carvings found in Greece date from the Bronze Age. Labyrinths and labyrinth-like images, ancient and modern, span the world through Europe, Russia, the Middle East, Turkey, Afghanistan, Pakistan,

India, Southeast Asia, and North America. Labyrinths are found in many religious traditions, including the Jewish mystical tradition of the Kabbalah or Tree of Life, the Native American Medicine Wheel, the Man in the Maze, and the Gothic Cathedrals of Europe (46), and by spiritual seekers, sacred and secular.

Awareness of the labyrinth faded more than 350 years ago. Until recently, Lauren Artress, priest, psychologist, and Pastor of Grace Cathedral in San Francisco, revived interest in the labyrinth through her research and teaching. In *Walking a Sacred Path: Rediscovering the Labyrinth as a Spiritual Practice*, she wrote the definitive source on this ancient mystical tool's history and spiritual evolution (1995/2006). She wrote:

> To walk a sacred path is to discover our inner sacred space: that care of feeling waiting to have life breathed into it through symbols, rituals, stories, and myths. Understanding the invisible world, the world of patterns, opens us up to the movement of the Spirit.
>
> (15)

In *The Faraway Nearby* (2013), Rebecca Solnit spoke of the labyrinth as a space where one perfects the art of unknowing. "There and back again took me ten or fifteen minutes by the clock. It was a time apart, symbolic time, a slow journey to the heart of the unknown and unknowable" (187). She continued, "The end of the journey through the labyrinth is not at the center, as is commonly supposed, but back at the threshold again: the beginning is also the real end. That is the home to which you return from the pilgrimage, the adventure" (188). As in the story of Ariadne's red thread, "You unspool the thread on the journey to the center. Then you rewind to escape" (188).

The thread motif woven throughout this chapter gives evidence of an outward sign of the inner presence of travelers on a pilgrimage. These travelers may be modern sojourners, mythical heroes, or heroines in a fairytale; all are seekers on a journey, known or unknown. The child's inner life of the Spirit is rarely discussed and less often studied. In the next chapter, Dr. Sole presents field research, including vignettes and narratives of children, that seek to understand the invisible, the unknown, and the immediate reality of spirituality in childhood.

Discoveries of the labyrinth and its practices throughout history, including Greek myths and fairytales, have advanced our understanding of the sacred invisible. Dr. Sole's knowledge and curiosity led her to find a labyrinth. In the following vignette, she shares her experience walking the labyrinth in her hometown.

The Labyrinth

> It's a warm sunny day in June when I pull up to the parking lot of a church in my town. It's a spot I visit often, a coffee house on the church property. I look down at my phone and open my email from the church's Minister of Care. "To find what you're looking for, follow the path behind the coffee house." Follow the path, I remind myself as I hop out of my car and pass by a mom with her toddler in a stroller; they smile.
>
> I peer over some hedges and spot exactly what I'm looking for. With no clear path, I clumsily scale over some bushes and find myself in front of a giant, circular stone labyrinth encircled by benches with a fire pit in the center. The stone pavers are faded from the sun, and weeds and grass sprout in between. The labyrinth is empty, yet I nervously search for the starting point, feeling self-conscious. I place my keys and phone on a bench, hit play on my wireless headphones, put on my baseball cap, and set off on the path. The walkway stones are reddish brown, and gray stones delineate the borders. Rather quickly, I hit a border and realize I did not begin at the beginning. The sun makes it difficult to distinguish between the path and borders. I finally spy the entrance, and I start again.
>
> For my first round, I attempt to quiet my mind. Still, I keep thinking about all of the obstacles: the pavers in need of repair, the giant tree growing into the outside circle, and the murky water inside the fire pit, blocking me from standing in the dead center. Is anyone watching me? I focus on the music in my ears.

I walk in and out of the labyrinth twice before removing the headphones. For my third trip, I notice birds chirping, a baby crying, cars whizzing by on the main street, and the beeping of a truck backing up nearby. I delight in the sounds and in finding new ways to bend and move my body around and under the branches of a hanging tree without losing my footing. When I reach the center, I shimmy my feet under the fire pit and stand there. By the fourth trip, I noticed two remarkable views in front of me: on one end, a large wooden cross, and the magnificent church steeple at the other. In my fifth and final trip, I vary my tempo, speeding up, slowing down, and locking into a rhythm.

At the end, I pause to reflect on walking the labyrinth: I traveled five circles, inward and outward; I learned that the center isn't the destination but part of the journey; I focused on the borders to direct me and show me that my journey isn't over; With each completion the path leads me back toward the center; and at some point, my mind stops racing and I lose all sense of time passing.

Only when I departed an hour later did I realize that I missed the pathway bordered by colorful flowering bushes when I first arrived. I thought about how beautiful the labyrinth is with its imperfections. Like my own journey of twists, turns, and obstacles. I am eager to see where the path takes me next time.

References

Artress, Lauren. *Walking a sacred path: Rediscovering the Labyrinth as a Spiritual Practice.* Penguin, 1995.

Eisner, Elliot. *Reimagining Schools: The Selected Works of Elliot Eisner.* Routledge, 2005.

Geertz, Clifford. *The Interpretation of Cultures.* Basic Books, 1973.

Higgins, Charlotte. *Red Thread: On Mazes and Labyrinths*. Random House, 2018.
Lawrence-Lightfoot, Sarah, and Jessica Hoffman Davis. *The Art and Science of Portraiture*. John Wiley and Sons, 2002.
MacDonald, George. *The Princess and the Goblin*. Blackie & Son, 2018.
Solnit, Rebecca. *The Faraway Nearby*. Penguin Books, 2013.
Strauss, Richard. *Ariadne auf Naxos*. Froemke, Susan, Gelb, Peter, and Haffe, Pat. Film producers. Metropolitan Opera Association, 1988.
Welty, Eudora. *One Writer's Beginnings*. Harvard University Press, 1983.

6

Pilgrimage

Meryl Sole

Threads, visible or invisible in allegories, parables, and myths, symbolize a spiritual journey. In my observations of young children in homes, classrooms, and travels, I witnessed instances of an inner state unknown and undocumented. Vignettes and narratives are presented here to reveal a colorful, ornate representation of children's spontaneous experiences of wonder, awe, and mystery. Each episode is constructed of threads weaving incidents into a story, a tale, or spinning a web.

Whenever I observe a child in an expressive mode, I seek ways to preserve the experience. I record details in each observation, filling my phone and computer with images and videos, including notes and emails to myself. My collection has grown exponentially over the past twelve years, with numerous handwritten journals containing my observations. Guided by a persistent need to know, I studied sociologist Sarah Lawrence-Lightfoot's (2002) research on portraiture to capture the "richness, complexity, and dimensionality" of children's expressions through descriptive and artful narrative.

Here, I present transcripts documenting children's engagement with, and awareness of, a spiritual phenomenon. This body of work focuses on recent findings organized into themes. In this chapter, I attend to my youngest daughter, a central figure in my research, and how she expressed surprise and wonder at everyday events. Throughout this book, I refer to her as "Meira," meaning enlightened or shining in Hebrew. During a ten-day trip to Israel with family, our Rabbi, and friends, I had an opportunity to observe and participate in her discoveries and insights into this sacred land. I noticed Meira engaging, exploring, and discovering everything natural and human-made, as in making a pilgrimage. In such a spiritual environment, I wondered what meaning it held for her as I watched and listened.

As a practicing Jew, I have always been intrigued by Jewish mysticism, particularly female mystics: Ines de Herra, the child mystic; Eva Frank, daughter of Jacob Joseph Frank, a self-proclaimed messiah and cultish leader of Frankism. Eva created a sub-cult, calling herself the female messiah; also, Maid of Ludmir, a female Hassidic Rebbe thought to grant miracles. These women's stories are filled with knowledge, visions, angels, dreams, and struggles against the norms of the society in which they lived.

For centuries, Jewish mystics have practiced Kabbalah, the tradition of Jewish mysticism, in search of truth and spiritual wisdom. Kabbalah translates to mean received wisdom. It is an ancient oral practice shrouded in mystery and secrets from an esoteric school of thought reserved for elite Torah scholars. In my studies of Jewish mysticism, I found the tenets of the Sefirot essential to my understanding. In brief, these are divine emanations, channels illuminating the soul and guiding the intellect, emotions, and actions. Through investigation, I learned the mystical qualities of wisdom, love, beauty, majesty, and kinship originating in childhood, characterizing children's freshness of spirit and openness to every new, novel stimulus with wonder, curiosity, and discovery.

These essential tenets of Jewish mysticism include ten Sefirot, divine emanations or channels illuminating the soul to guide intellect, emotion, and action. This emanation is a "mysterious process through which God allows something of himself to flow into our infinite world" (Jacobs, 1984, 91). These Sefirot include God's will, understanding, wisdom, power, lovingkindness, beauty, splendor, victory, foundation, and sovereignty. In Hebrew, this correlates to Keter, Binah, Hokhmah, Gevurah, Hesed, Tifret, Hod, Netzah, Yesod, and Malkhut. The Kabbalistic

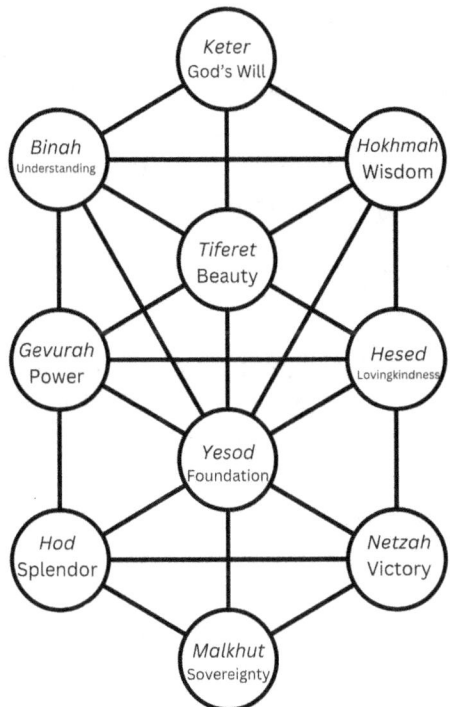

FIGURE 6.1 The Kabbalistic Tree

tree, a tool for understanding the metaphysical, spiritual world, illustrates these divine emanations that bridge the "Ein Sof," the unknowable God, with our realm. The right side of the tree shows Sefirot Hesed, the male representation of the divine attributes of compassion, generosity, and mercy. The left side represents the female attributes of the Sefirah of Din, the awesomeness of God in judgment, might, and power. In the tree's center, we find a balance of Tiferet, mercy, and justice. As illustrated in Figure 6.1, each sphere is interconnected, allowing light to flow from one to the next through these interlinked paths.

Shalom Israel

In December of 2022, my family traveled to Israel from the United States on a mission with our synagogue. Over ten days,

35 participants and our Rabbi explored our holy land's different sites and mystical villages. My husband, our twelve-year-old daughter, our seven-year-old daughter, and their maternal and paternal grandmothers participated. Early in the trip, I began documenting Meira's experiences with photographs and field notes recorded daily on my iPhone.

Intuition and Discovery

> It is colder than I imagined December in Jerusalem. The sun shines brightly, but we are bundled in our coats with the wind whipping around us. As the mama of the youngest member of this large group, I feel anxious about how my little one will handle jet lag and how the teenagers will treat her. After a long bus ride, we arrive at the Bet Guvrin National Park outside Jerusalem to participate in an archaeological "dig for a day" at King Herod's ancestral home, a UNESCO World Heritage Site.
>
> We descend the steep rock steps into a dimly lit cave, and I grasp Meira's little hand tightly, worried she might fall. Looking around me, I pull my hair into my baseball cap, fearing what insects and creatures might hide. Meira does not seem to share my fears. She runs straight to the piles of spades and shovels, ready to roll up her sleeves and start digging. In minutes, she is covered from head to toe with dust. Her ponytail is red with soil, and her nails are caked.
>
> Every few minutes, I am interrupted from my careful digging (trying not to destroy my manicure) by shouts of "Mama, look!" or "I found another!" Meira is exuberant with each discovery. For her, every pottery shard is a piece of treasure, a precious gem from long ago. "I wonder what this piece was part of?" "Who used it?" "What was it for?" Her questions are as endless as are her joyous exclamations.
>
> After an hour passed, we were asked to return our tools and ascend above ground. Prying the spade from Meira's grasp, I promise her more adventures at the cave's entrance. She leads the way back up the stairs to an area where we are instructed to sift the leftover dirt to find any remaining

artifacts. Aha! There are more mysterious treasures! Another mom (a stranger at the time and now a dear family friend) offers to partner with Meira for the sifting. Happily, Meira accepts the invitation. She shakes and sifts the soil with her new buddy for any artifacts. They laugh and squeal in minutes, adding more dirt to their soiled clothes.

The dig leader ushers us to a small pavilion when the work is done. We gather in a semicircle and listen to stories about ancient people and their way of life. The guide tells us about the "Heliodoros stele" artifact (28 lines inscribed on limestone) recently discovered on this site. He passes around a photo of the artifact encased in a plastic sleeve protector. Meira studies the picture in great detail.

We depart for the city, eager to rest on the bus ride back to the Old City—a moment to breathe before Shabbat services at the Western Wall.

In observance of Shabbat, most sites, restaurants, and businesses are closed on Saturday. The adults are excited to learn that the Israel Museum is still open, perhaps with an opportunity to see the famous Dead Sea Scrolls. We head there, much to the chagrin of our children, who would likely prefer the indoor pool at the hotel or a playground. Everyone is tired and hungry. Meira is cranky and repeatedly asks for a snack. I rifle through my purse, looking for an old lollipop or bag of gummies, but no luck.

The museum exhibits seem endless, one ancient bowl and pitcher after another. Just as my patience is at a breaking point, I hear, "Mama, I found it! The treasure!" Excited with pride and glee, Meira led our family to a museum exhibit of the original Heliodoros artifact. Meira recognized it from the replica at the archeological dig the day before. I watch as she admires her discovery. Her eyes are wide open, sparkling with joy and satisfaction. Meira is attuned to everything around her, using her mind and body to immerse herself in new surroundings. Intuition draws her to artifacts hidden from the rest of us yet in plain sight to her. She radiates joy, insight, and wisdom, sharing her discoveries and their importance with her family.

Spontaneous Musical Devotion

Our group gathers at the Western Wall on our first Shabbat in Israel on the fifth night of Hanukah, The Festival of Lights. Called the Kotel or Wailing Wall, this holy site is the remaining wall of the second temple in the Old City of Jerusalem. It is the closest place to the Temple Mount, where Jews can pray. I hold Meira's hand as we walk through winding ancient streets. As the sun sets, we gaze at the changing colors of the sky, bathing everyone and everything in a warm golden glow. We approach the plaza surrounded by thousands of fellow Jews, all coming together to welcome the Sabbath. The air is chilly, but there is a feeling of warmth. The hum of chanting encircles us, and the prayers of different groups at different intervals create a drone of sound. We form a circle as the Rabbi leads our Shabbat service. We share melodies and prayers carried from home with our brothers and sisters: "L'Cha Dodi" (Welcoming the Sabbath Bride), The "Shema" *Hear O Israel the Lord is our God, The Lord is One*, "V'Shamru" (Guarding of Shabbat). At home and here, we conclude the service by holding each other and singing "Shalom Aleichem." *Peace be Upon You*. Meira rarely joins in singing and chanting; instead, she quietly watches and absorbs the service.

In this sacred place, my husband and I are moved to tears, so honored to recite the Mourner's Kaddish prayer for our late fathers. Meira grasps my hand even firmer, sending love and comfort. Afterward, we return to the hotel for our Shabbat dinner. The mood is quiet and sweet. Meira's hand has not left mine.

The following evening, after a busy day filled with sightseeing, I help Meira prepare for bedtime. I hear it from the bathroom, where I'm cleaning up dirty clothes left on the floor! "V'shamru, v'nei Yisrael et ha Shabbat, La'asot et ha Shabbat l'dorotam brit olam." Meira is in bed, wrapped in a warm fuzzy towel, singing to herself. The prayer means that *the people of Israel shall keep Shabbat, observing Shabbat throughout the ages as a covenant for all time*. On this journey to her homeland, Meira joins the people of Israel in an ancient and sacred prayer in her own time and way. Through spontaneous chanting, Meira connects herself, L'Dor Va Dor, to her family, her congregation, and generations of Jews.

Found Treasure

Leaving the archeological dig, Meira smuggles a large white stone with a perfectly circular hole onto the tour bus, thinking about *How this hole got there. Is this rock special? Maybe it is magical.* At the hotel, I asked, "Why is your jacket so heavy?"

I already know the answer to my question. This smuggling has happened before. Last year, at the airport, returning home from another trip—unbeknownst to me and the rest of the family—Meira had packed multiple large tennis ball-sized rocks in the outside pocket of her carry-on backpack. How did it clear airport security? Reaching into the pockets of her light pink puff coat, I pull out handfuls of rocks, stones, and leaves. Meira explains, "These are my treasures. I am collecting them." The treasure hunter persists.

Two days later, Meira and I, my mother, and a friend stand at the entrance to the Jerusalem Biblical Zoo. The sound of laughing children is all around, yet thinking of the rest of our group at the Yad Vashem Holocaust Museum, I feel a heaviness around me, knowing Meira is too young to go there.

We set off for a Zoo adventure. Not ten feet onto the path, Meira stops to pick up a long stick with a pinecone attached. I think to myself: *Where did this come from? How can the pinecone be connected in this way?* To Meira, it's a magic wand, another treasure in her collection. I watch as she takes the wand and carries it wherever she goes. Amazingly, a year and a half later, I discovered that wilted wand in a special box in our playroom at home. Treasure saved.

Spirit Animals

Grandma loves penguins, so we head to the penguin exhibit. Behind the glass display window, we watch adorable tuxedo-wearing birds hopping from rocks and swimming in a large pool. "Look how cute they are!," Meira squeals. Then, with a lift of her magic pinecone wand,

Meira grabs the attention of a single penguin that mysteriously connects with her. With her wand, Meira directs the little bird across the rocks into the pool and back out again. More penguins join in, going back and forth, back and forth following Meira, the Magical Penguin Conductor. Quietly I record the episode on my phone, trying to avoid interruption. Meira and Grandma are howling in delight. We stay with the penguins for a long time.

This is just the beginning of Meira's interactions with animals. Days later, a particularly friendly and quick speckled gray cat waits for us outside our room at a Kibbutz Kfar Blum. To my horror, the cat dashes into Meira's room and hides until two hotel employees come to remove it. The cat and friends wait for Meira to leave them snacks and treats each night. Sometimes, she offers bits of leaves and branches from among her treasure collections. Meira calls these healthy "nature salads," a specialty dish that makes another appearance later.

In addition to penguins and cats, she lures a flock of peacocks. A few days later, in the parking lot at Tel Dan Nature Reserve in the Upper Galilee of Northern Israel, our entire tour group stops to see Meira commune with the colorful birds. "Show us your tails!," Meira says as she leads the peacocks around the parking lot. Meira's interconnection with animals signifies the divine emanation of Hesed or God's love for all his creatures.

Nature Salad

"Can you reach that leaf for me?," Meira asks a teenage group member. Her small hand is outstretched and struggling to grasp the colorful leaf. Her helper becomes a new friend. She follows Meira and helps her fill her baseball cap with berries, leaves, flowers, and rocks. Soon, other teenagers join in, helping her craft a "nature salad." While on board for a sunset cruise on the Sea of Galilee, Meira prepares the salad. She removes her barrettes and uses them as salad tongs to share her salad with everyone. She visits tour members eager and willing to partake in her treasure-filled salad. A grandma from another family is interested in playing with Meira and her nature salad. Her daughter-in-law told me it was out of character for her to do so. The passengers are charmed, and they take photos of the mini chef and her salad. They post "Door Dash" text messages to promote the drama: "Come and get your nature salad, fast and friendly delivery!" For the duration of the boat trip, people continue playing together with the nature salad, an expression of Hesed and lovingkindness unites the group.

Mercy Fish

A week into our ten-day tour, everyone feels tired from nonstop sightseeing. Throughout, we have become more comfortable with each other, and the children have bonded together, making Meira the mascot of their group. Our bus pulls into the Golan Heights winery, an idyllic setting in a stunning vineyard. As we enter the chic, modern visitors center, the Rabbi announces, "Enjoy yourselves, grown-ups! I'll watch the kids!" An offer we cannot refuse. He hustles the pack of teens and children, including Meira, outside to a playground. What a sweet and generous offer. I am happy to get help where I can.

Grown-ups visit the processing center inside the winery and sample several wine varieties in the beautiful tasting room. Now relaxed, we board the bus. Rabbi leans over to me and says, "I have a story for you..." Knowing my interest in observing children, the Rabbi regales me with a tale of the "mercy fish." The story begins with Rabbi and Meira taking a short walk around the vineyard property. Soon, they approach a small pond where several big children are

> throwing rocks and poking sticks at a little fish in the water. They are much bigger than seven-year-old Meira, who is petite for her age. Many of them speak only Hebrew, which Meira does not understand. Despite the challenges, Meira quickly comes to the defense of the little fish. "They may be bigger than me, but that is the only difference. The fish deserves to live." She bends over the water, removes the leaves and sticks within reach, and then chases the mean children away from the area. She stands guard over the fish for some time should they come back. Rabbi recounts the story with great pride and amazement. Little Meira saved the fish! Such bravery in the face of risk and uncertainty expresses Tiferet, the harmonization of love and power.

Penguins, cats, peacocks, and now a fish. Meira's rapport with all living creatures shows undeniable mercy and compassion. In Kabbalah, the Tzelem, or animal soul, is one of a person's two souls. Tzelem is the soul that gives life to the physical body. In the Tanya, an early work of Hasidic philosophy written to guide Jewish spiritual life, Tzelem is known as the source of the animal soul and innate Jewish characteristics such as kindness and empathy.

Mud Gloves

What a day. When our bus arrives at the Dead Sea, we barely have enough time to recover and dry out from the torrential rains atop Masada. The sign before us reads, "Welcome to the Lowest Place on Earth." Our tour guide leads us to single-gender changing rooms. Meira takes my hand as we enter a modest, open changing area. The aroma is strong and unpleasant, and Meira bolts for the exit. The chance of her changing into a swimsuit in that room is zero, even though the outside temperature is barely 50 degrees Fahrenheit. My mother and oldest daughter waste no time jumping into bathing suits and collecting tiny thread-bare towels at the entrance. They are off and running, barely able to contain their excitement. Within seconds, they are floating in the saltiest body of water on the planet, a sea so dense and brackish that it cannot sustain any life. Ironically, this barren sea is full of rich, healthful minerals.

With the other grandma napping on the tour bus, Meira, my husband, and I stand at the shoreline, bundled in our hats and coats, watching the few brave souls swim and float together in the ice-cold water. Slowly, Meira inches closer to the water, first with a few fingers, then an arm. Soon, her shoes and socks are off, her pants rolled above her knees, and her beige hooded sweatshirt with pink and purple hearts pushed above her elbow. When she begins to cover herself in mud, I think, how am I going to clean her off? But her enjoyment assuages my worrying.

With her hands and arms caked with mud, she models them for us like elegant opera evening gloves. She laughs and squeals with delight playing at the shore's edge long after everyone else has left to change into their street clothes. I glimpse at my watch and realize it is time to go. Like clockwork, the skies open up, and we are drenched again. Thankfully, the mud washes off Meira's arms and feet back to the earth below. Kabbalists consider the Dead Sea a representation of the Sefirot, Malchut, meaning that exaltedness and humility are joined together in this rare place, just as life and death are joined.

On Sacred Ground

When God gave the Jewish people the gift of the Torah at Mount Sinai, God instructed us to build an altar of the earth that is simple and humble. At each site, Meira creates sacred markings in dedication. For her, the purpose of each natural item is not only to add to her collection of treasures but to create and mark exceptional experiences and events. Meira reminds me of the Jewish tradition of visitors marking gravestones by leaving rocks atop them.

Meira's sacred inscriptions symbolize, "I was here."

Chapter Notes

Professor, sound artist, philosopher, and musician Marcel Cobussen writes extensively on his spiritual encounters with music, sharing vivid and evocative descriptions of his experiences. Whether meditating on George Crumb's *Black Angels* or J.S. Bach's *Passions*, he uses rich, descriptive language to illustrate physical and emotional experiences. Cobussen's gift for naming the unnamable and describing what happens in his body and mind inspired my research and guided my descriptions of what I observed in children.

References

Jacobs, Louis. *The Book of Jewish Belief*. Behrman House, 1984.

Lawrence-Lightfoot, Sarah, and Jessica Hoffman Davis. *The Art and Science of Portraiture*. John Wiley and Sons, 2002.

7

One With God

Meryl Sole

In the previous chapter, as a participant observer, I shared my young daughter Meira's mystical experiences in the Holy Land. For Meira, all of Israel was sacred. Her experience was enhanced through interactions with family and everyone in our pilgrimage group, including older children, clergy, and other adults. Analysis showed the importance of community support for a child's spiritual discoveries through love, trust, and care.

Here, I present more narratives from my fieldwork of children with families, individual children, and children at play. When humans exhibit sacred characteristics, they embody God within themselves. Our godly actions are demonstrations of the holy and are most present through our connection to others. God, at the core of being, is deep within our relationships, in our expressions of goodness and love with our children, families, friends, and the world around us.

Figure 7.1 depicts children's spiritual interconnectedness through concentric circles with God at the center.

Inspired by the art of narrative quilting, I present the following collection of children's vignettes that constitute a story quilt, telling the tale of children's spirituality; each episode is woven together with sacred threads.

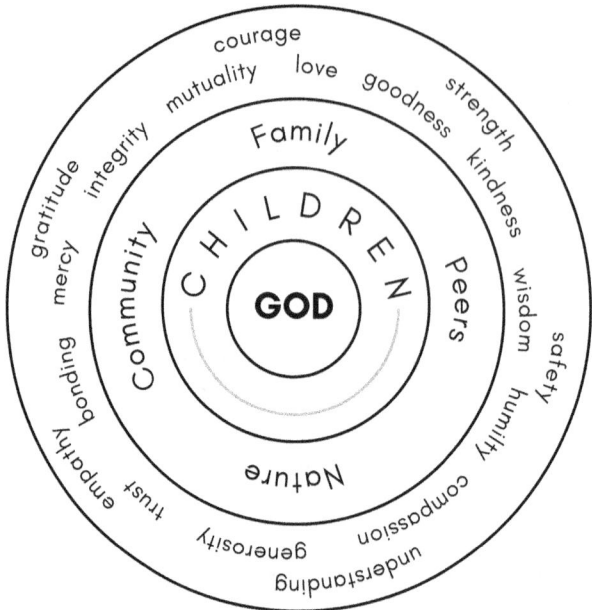

FIGURE 7.1 Children's Spiritual Interconnectedness

Thread 1, Children and Families

In the first three vignettes, we see children engage with their families where spiritual threads of intuition, wisdom, focus, devotion, empathy, and grace become visible.

Japanese Journey

> A ten-day journey to Japan with its sights, sounds, and tastes was an exotic experience for my family compared to daily life in America. A few days into our adventure, we visit an art museum in the bustling city of Tokyo. One of the exhibits, called "Team Lab Planets," is an interactive display designed to be experienced in the company of others where one immerses their body to "become one with the world." Our family begins in the Infinite Crystal Universe, a maze of ever-changing three-dimensional crystal lights inviting us to run, hide, and play among them. Next, we discover the

water area, where we wade into a warm pool surrounded by projections of neon-colored Koi fish that move and change as we interact. My nine-year-old daughter creates a game by dancing through the pool, chasing and catching fish that ultimately turn into flowers when touched.

Next, we move to a dome-shaped dark room called Floating in the Universe of Falling Flowers. We join many strangers lying on our backs in the center of the room on a mirrored floor. My older daughter lies next to me as the younger one reclines with her head in my lap. She does not move from this position for almost 45 minutes as we watch stunning projections of flowers budding, blooming, and falling away all around us while enchanting music fills the space. After a while, my younger daughter rolls over in my lap and says, "Mama, the art is trying to tell us something. It's the story of a year." She continues, "This is about life, being born, growing, and dying. But it all repeats itself. The world is beautiful. The different colored flowers are different personalities that make each person special. You are strong enough to do anything." I smile, marveling at her wisdom. Meira feels the life force in her soul and knows a moment of transformation. As we exit Floating in the Universe of Falling Flowers, we find a sign, "A season of year flowers bloom and change with time, life spreads out into the universe … Flowers grow, bud, bloom, and in time, the pedals fall, and the flowers wither and die. The cycle of birth and death continues for perpetuity."

As we pass through a Torii gate toward a Shinto temple, Meira's energy and behavior are even more spirited. She is enchanted as she learns the traditional Shinto rituals of hand and mouth cleansing, bowing, and making offerings. Taking each task seriously, she completes each ritual "exactly right." On our way to visit a shrine in Tokyo, Meira picks up a long branch and attaches a leaf to the top. To her, it's a magic wand. She carries this treasure for several days until it is time to pack it safely in her suitcase to bring home.

Our adventure included visits to Buddhist temples to engage in rituals guided by monks. At one temple, our family receives instruction from the presiding monk on the ritual of the tea ceremony. Meira is captivated by the dance-like, choreographed steps scooping the matcha and pouring the water. She closely observes as the monk uses rhythmic brushstrokes to blend the powder as he turns the cup clockwise to serve and sip. He notices Meira's interest and invites her to learn the routine. Meira is now fully immersed in the ritual and deeply focused on the process. A day later, we visit another temple for guided meditation. We learn to sit still, hold our hands and remain in absolute stillness for fifteen minutes. The monk guiding us is astounded that such a small child could engage so deeply in meditation. He offers our group a second meditation. While some adults decline, Meira is eager to participate again. As before, she maintains focus and stillness absorbed into a meditative state.

Sunbeam Dancer

Colors of brown, orange, yellow, red, and gold decorate the ornate church in Munich. There are paintings from the floor to ceiling and across every wall. The surfaces are covered in stone. Smiling angels and scary skulls are carved into the walls. The glow of golden decorations fills the space, there is so much to absorb I don't know where to look first. Art is everywhere. I sit in the pews, to take it all in, when I notice a small blonde girl about three years old. Her mommy holds her hand tightly. She yearns to break away and touch one of the many sculptures covered in gold. She sits between Mommy and Daddy as he points to the organ, altar, and ceiling. Mommy takes her hand. Walking back toward the entrance, her parents stop to talk with a stranger, they speak Spanish. The mother is still holding her child's hand. With attention to the child, I pause to watch her. Looking towards the entrance, a ray of golden sunshine shining directly on her. Only the child notices it, as if it is just for her. She takes her free hand and slowly rotates her wrist. Small circles grow as tiny fingers gracefully float and dance in the glorious warmth of the sunbeam. The adults conclude their conversation, Mommy tugs her daughter's hand, pulling her towards the exit. The dance ends.

I Am With God

One afternoon, I visit a third-grade classroom where children were given a writing assignment to complete a poem with these prompts: I am___, I wonder___, I hear___, I see ___, I want to be___ and, I dream___. A beginning-of-the-school-year activity encourages children's self-expression and provides their teacher with knowledge and understanding of each student. Results are posted on a bulletin board. I read poems about happy children, flowers, dreams of unicorns, and one about being a doctor. Following the prompts, each child revealed things personal and important to them. I find myself typing notes about their poetry into my phone. A few children expressed deeply held spiritual beliefs, referencing God seen and heard in dreams. They write about understanding the world and seeing and believing in the Divine. These child poets identify as kind, strong, and happy.

Thread 2, Children with Others

The following vignettes show children engaging with their families and other members of their communities who foster trust, safety, and support, revealing expressions of love and belonging.

A Mystical Vision

"You probably won't believe me because it sounds too crazy," a teenage girl remarks, talking about a magical experience that she could not explain. I assure her that I will believe her as she launches into a memory from four years prior.

The family gathered at synagogue on a typical Friday night to celebrate Shabbat. At nine years old, she's familiar with the liturgy and order of the prayers in the service, able to anticipate what comes next. She sits in between her parents and close to her sister. The congregation is still seated as they begin *Lehak Dodi*, a prayer to welcome the Sabbath as a beautiful bride in their midst. The melody is upbeat and festive, and the refrain is easy to sing along in with. The Hebrew translates to "Let us go, my beloved, to greet the bride/the Sabbath presence, let us welcome." In the final verse, the rabbi tells everyone to stand and face the entrance to the room. The congregation gently bows at the words, *Boi khalah boi khalah*, meaning "Come O Bride! Come, O Bride!" This is where the girl sees something extraordinary. Flowing from the entrance, an ethereal figure is clad in a flowing white garment. The aberration floats into the room and onto the bimah, encircling the rabbi through the crescendo of the final refrain until the prayer concludes. When they finish and are invited to sit back down, the apparition disappears as quickly as it first emerged. Witnessing this, the girl feels no fear, only a sense of calm and warmth, and emotions of happiness and surprise. The girl is certain she is not imagining things; she knows that it happened. Four years after experiencing the vision, she recalls it with great detail and certainty, expressing some hesitation and concern that no one will believe her. Yet she is certain it was real.

A Shabbat Wonder

She looks about two years old, slightly wobbly on her feet, and constantly in motion; her two little pigtails flop as she moves. She wears a fancy pink flower dress and party shoes, chosen for this special occasion. Her outfit appears a little uncomfortable, but it does not restrain her from bouncing about and exerting her exuberance. For adults, a Friday night Shabbat service is brief, only 45 minutes from start to end, and I think about how this time frame can feel like an eternity for a parent with a small child. However, this little girl seems unfazed as she happily climbs from lap to lap in the front row. First, her mother, then her father, then her older brother, the honored guest and bar mitzvah boy. She alternates dance moves with hugs and kisses, sharing her love and embrace with each new partner.

The atmosphere in the sanctuary is warm and glowing. It is a hot June night when the sun is still out and sends its rays beaming through the stained-glass windows on the bimah. It is a night of many celebrations. In addition to the impending coming-of-age ceremony, the congregation is gathering to celebrate PRIDE, an inclusivity Sabbath featuring additional singers and musicians. I find myself distracted from the prayers, intensely watching this little girl. She appears restless and ready to move on from the seats.

The moment arrives; the cantor reaches for her guitar and begins to strum with a gentle, melodic prayer. The little girl breaks free from her mother and begins her journey to the cantor, crossing the row of steps that separate her from the front. My heart begins to race, wondering if Mom and Dad will grab or restrain her. To my delight, the adults remain seated, and a giant smile spreads across the rabbi's face. The cantor continues to sing, and the little girl slowly approaches. Her mouth is open, and her eyes are wide. I am frozen in anticipation. She makes it all the way up the steps and stands in front of the cantor, incredibly still, absorbing the prayer. I quickly shift my focus from the pair to the rest of the congregation. Kindness, smiles, and expressions of joy[abound]. Just as the[little] girl becomes transfixed by the music, we are mesmerized by her, joining in her expression[s] of wonder and awe.

Finding Her Sacred Voice

The sanctuary is empty for a Friday night Shabbat service. It's mid-August, and most congregants are either traveling or staying home to avoid the heat, humidity, and intermittent thunderstorms. My husband and I sit in our usual seats with our youngest daughter; our older girl is still away at sleepaway camp. Dressed up in a sundress, our nine-year-old sits quietly in between us, the only child in the room. As usual, she refuses to hold or open the *Siddur* (prayerbook) and does not sing along, although she is familiar with the liturgy, having attended this service regularly for years. She sits quietly, fidgeting with a bracelet, sometimes reaching for my hand to hold. I wrap my arm around her, and she snuggles in close for a hug. Mid-way through the 45-minute service, the Rabbi signals to her to come up onto the *bimah* with him. As is customary in our congregation, young children are invited up for the kiddush, the prayer over the wine. Each week, she approaches the Rabbi, who lovingly pinches her cheek and whispers something to her that always induces a smile. Proudly, she holds up the kiddush cup as the Rabbi, Cantor, and congregation sing together. She does not mouth a word but stands silently, cup in hand and arm outstretched. The elders in the congregation praise her cup-holding skills and delight in her participation, referring to her as the "Statue of Liberty" of the kiddush. This is her role, and she welcomes it with honor and cheerfulness. But tonight, I realize she has been called up early. The rabbi announces, "Tonight you will join me in the *Oshe Shalom*," the prayer for peace. The Rabbi places a hand-held microphone in front of her mouth, and together they begin to sing, *Oseh shalom bimromav, hu ya'aseh shalom aleinu v'al kol Yisra'eil v'imru Amein* meaning: He who makes peace in His heights may He make peace upon us and upon all Israel. Amen. Her voice is small yet powerful as she sings each Hebrew word perfectly. She and the Rabbi clap together during silent pauses in the rhythm, hitting their hands together in pat-a-cake style. There are giggles of delight from the small group of adults. My husband and I stand still, our mouths open in surprise as we make eye contact. The rabbi's smile beams from ear to ear. She *has* been listening and absorbing in her own way all these years. The gentle invitation is just right, and the room's love and trust create a space for her prayer to soar.

Rock Band

Almost two weeks into a South American adventure with our extended family, we arrive at the Petrohué Waterfalls in Chile. The falls stem from the Osorno Volcano between Todos los Santos and Llanquihue Lake. The scenery is majestic, and the volcano is massive and imposing, covered in snow, even though it is summer. We wear T-shirts as we bask in the warm sun. After hiking through the national park area, we end up on a beach surrounded by dark sand and covered in volcanic rock. The adults continue to walk along the shoreline while my daughters and their cousins sit and rest on large stones. It is windy, our hair blows about. My husband and I walk together, hand in hand. Even though the wind is roaring, something catches my ear: the distinct sound of repeated rhythmic clicks and singing. I look back on the beach to find my older daughter, my niece, and the tour guide watching my youngest daughter. With a stone in one hand and a stick in another, Meira bangs them together and chants, *"Sticks and stones, it's time to roam."* She invites the older girls and the tour guide to join her in forming a band. The new members accompany her singing, all keeping the beat as she grooves and dances to her spontaneous "rock song." The older members intuitively know how to play a supportive role; they never sing or take the lead. When Meira finishes the song, the band breaks up. Others throw their stick and stones back on the beach, but Meira saves her "instruments" and carries them as treasures for the rest of the trip.

Thread 3, Together, Children Transcend Differences

The following section features children interacting with each other—threads of kindness, goodness, empathy, compassion, and belonging.

Symbols of Belief

In a third-grade art class, children are asked to create a drawing using only four colors and any color combinations. In the first picture, two girls who are mirror images of each other are holding hands. One has tears streaming down her face and the other is smiling. Each girl wears a religious symbol around her neck. The girl who cries wears a cross and the other girl wears a Star of David. In the center of their heads is a dark black, upside-down triangle. Resting on the platform of the shape is a sad, gray person. The artist interprets her art, "The girl on the right is me. She is crying because she remembers a scary time when she fell off a huge rock and cut herself so badly, she had to go to the ER to get stitches." She says that she is the smaller girl laying on a field of black representing her memory and the girl on the left is comforting her.

The child-artist's mother wondered about the religious symbols since her family does not practice a religion. The mother surmises, "[My daughter] had them wearing a cross and a star to show that everyone is a person and the same underneath. The girl on the left was reaching out and comforting her as a fellow human, not considering that they were different religions." When mom asked her daughter if she identifies as Christian, her child simply replies, "I believe in God."

Playmates in Paradise

It's a hot and balmy Saturday night as we arrive at a lovely local restaurant on West Bay in Grand Cayman for a celebratory dinner on our final night in paradise. Having dined at this charming and festive place two days earlier, we decide to return. Meira says, "Let's go back and see Bobo the Iguana." We arrive at the restaurant relaxed after a sun-kissed day on the beach, swimming, snorkeling, and playing together. The host seats us at a table facing the dock with a beautiful view of the sunset. There was a giant tarpon swimming in the waters below us and Bobo the Iguana sleeping in his cage on the dock. We enjoy our meals and tropical cocktails, while a two-piece Reggae band plays "Saturday night, it's Saturday night," accompanied by the voices of small children. Intrigued by the song and curious about the children, my daughter and I leave Grandma at the table and head over to investigate.

We find four sisters dancing and singing in front of the band. Immediately, they spot Meira in her pink sundress. The youngest sister called Luna is barely two years old. She runs up and tightly hugs Meira with love. Each sister takes turns hugging Meira. What a warm and most joyful greeting to a new friend, "How old are you?" they ask.

These children from the island are thrilled to welcome their newest playmate and Meira, who is just as thrilled, responds without hesitation. Lovely to see there are no strangers among the children by age or race. One sister exclaims, "Let's go see the fish!" they grab Meira's hand and head off to the edge of the dock, laughing and playing together on the pier. At the end of this beautiful Saturday night, we bid farewell to our new friends with endless hugs, waves, and smiles.

The Fountain

On a hot July afternoon, after solo sightseeing all over Munich, I end up at the famous *Frauenkirche*. I need a break after exploring the cathedral and placing my foot over the infamous "devil's footprint" at the entrance. I find myself in the town square directly across from the church at an interesting fountain encircled by amphitheater-style steps. These steps are crowded with people eating lunch, having a coffee, chatting, and watching children play. I find a small vacant piece of real estate and crack open a cold bottle of ice water. Much to my delight, a spectacular show is about to unfold right before me.

The fountain is constructed of bronze-colored sculptures like mushrooms or lily pads jutting from the water. Children of all ages are barefoot inside the fountain, although I notice that the water is somewhat murky and green. They hop from mushroom to mushroom and splash around to cool off from the heat.

I notice pairs of siblings and children of many backgrounds and cultures speaking multiple languages. They all play together, communicating through gestures. and showing the rules of the games without words. They play games of chase and follow the leader. When the game becomes too simple, they up the ante skipping over one, then two mushrooms at a time.

I spot two siblings, a brother and a younger sister. The older brother has stripped off his shoes, socks, and shirt; he is ready for a day at the pool! His younger sister discovers a tree branch that suddenly is transformed into a walking cane; she is an old lady hobbling across the mushroom path. Then her brother takes the stick; like magic, it is now a fishing pole; much to their excitement, he reels in a ton of imaginary fish. Their drama with the stick continues as a small toddler does a "bear crawl" across their path, without interrupting the episode.

I sit for over an hour among the children and watch, dogs hop into the fountain. Occasionally, an adult takes off their shoes and joins in. I return the following day to this fountain theatre in the shadow of the great cathedral ready to watch new games and dramas unfold.

In this chapter, I captured children's voices, visions, actions, and spiritual experiences. As a participant observer, I organized extensive notes and video recordings from my observations and transcribed them into narratives. It was helpful to envision each vignette as related parts connecting to a whole story, like threads within a patchwork quilt. Creating and documenting narratives ultimately revealed themes for constructing a central story. This approach is a model for researchers, teachers, parents, and others seeking to understand the elusive nature of children's spirituality.

Chapter Notes

Researchers Hay and Nye (2006) propose children's *relational consciousness* as spiritual engagement through the contexts of child–people, child–self, child–world, and child–God. Conversely, my perspective focuses on God at the core of children's spiritual engagements and relationships.

Concentric circles to plot out relationships have ancient origins. Egyptian philosopher Heracles of Alexandria (1st or 2nd century) applied the geometric figure of concentric circles to represent humanity with the human mind at the center and radiating to family, extended family, local groups, citizens, countrymen, and society. Nicolaus Copernicus (1473–1543) applied concentric circles to explain his heliocentric theory, placing the sun at the center point of the universe with widening circles of the earth and the planets. For example, when a rock is tossed into a lake, ripples radiate from the point of impact, resulting in concentric circles from the center.

Narrative quilts have a rich history of storytelling and preserving the past through the art of quilting. Quilts that illustrate stories of the Bible, Native American experience, Appalachian life, Abolition, and the Underground Railroad are all examples of an artistic medium used to communicate life stories. Modern-day artist Faith Ringgold (1996) was known for her painted story quilts, most notably *Tar Beach*, which tells the story of a young girl dreaming atop her family's Harlem apartment building.

References

Hay, Daniel, and Rebecca Nye. *The Spirit of the Child*. Jessica Kingsley Publishers, 2006.
Ringgold, Faith. *Tar Beach*. Dragonfly Books, 1996.

8

Children of Faith

Danette Littleton

If we are to recognize children's spirituality, we need discernment and enlightenment in ourselves. Families pass their faith traditions of belonging, security, and trust to their children. When we rediscover spiritual experiences from our childhood, we may better understand those of our children. Listen to children's voices below, taken from a collection, *A Faith Like Mine: A Celebration of the World's Religions Through the Eyes of Children* (2005).

Buddhism

From the United States, Zoe said, "Buddhism is very peaceful. My brother and I chant to overcome challenges. We also chant for the happiness of others. When friends ask what the altar is, I say it's where we pray" (28).

From Japan, Maiko said,

> I live in a temple because both my parents work as priests. My father began to teach me how to recite a sutra (scripture) called O-kyo when I was three years old. Buddhism

teaches us to be aware of ourselves and to review our attitudes again and again.

(28)

Judaism

From France, Benjamin said, "My soul is a little ghost inside me."

> I'm Benjamin, and I'm nine. My faith allows me to get in touch with my soul. I go to a synagogue in a beautiful square in Paris. Every Sunday, I study the Torah there. It's really interesting. During the festival of Hanukkah, we remember a special miracle that happened a long time ago.
>
> (46)

From the United States, Erin said,

> Fridays are my favorite nights. Other nights are a little crazy for my family, but on Shabbat, we all sit down for a nice meal. We light candles and ask for God's blessings. My faith in God helps me heal my problems and answer my questions. This year, I had my Bat Mitzvah. I wanted people to see me for who I am and my dedication to becoming a Jewish adult.
>
> (48)

Christianity

From Italy:

> My name is Antonino, and I am ten. Soccer is my favorite sport because it is a team game, and many children can play together. The church I go to is a Catholic church in the square in our village. The thing that interests me most about my faith is Jesus' commandment that we love and

forgive each other. This year, I received the sacrament of First Communion.

(54)

From Ghana:

My name is Hannah. I am eight years old, and I have a younger brother and sister. My faith makes me feel happy and excited. My favorite celebration is Christmas. My family shares with each other by buying presents, having fun, and eating food. Every week, we go to church to worship. The best part of the service is Sunday School. That's where I do my Bible studies. I also like the preaching because the pastor makes me laugh. We listen and try to do good so that our faith will help us every day.

(60)

Islam

From Morocco:

I am Rachid, and I am nine years old. I like playing soccer and listening to music. Someday, I want to visit the city of Marrakech. Islam is the religion I know about. It teaches me how to be good with people and behave in a nice way. It only takes me five minutes to walk to the mosque nearby. I often go there during the week and always on Friday because it is a holy day. The Five Pillars are important because they are the things all Muslims must do to show faith and respect to Allah.

(64)

From Dubai:

My name is Mohammed, and I'm 13 years old. My faith makes me feel peaceful and secure. I go to mosque every day. Friday prayers are especially important, and all men must pray in the mosque. My father, brother, and I never miss this. My favorite place in the mosque is standing in the first three rows behind the imam because these are the people that Allah will be looking at. One of the things that Muslims must do is to worship Allah by going on Hajj, a pilgrimage to Mecca. Hajj is one of the Five Pillars. Eid-al-Adha is the feast to mark the end of this special journey.

(70)

In these brief autobiographies, common threads emerge in the children's voices about the meaningfulness of family in spiritual formation. They expressed joy and interest in studying scripture and learning about their faith traditions. They spoke of love, forgiveness, and the happiness of others. Each child described participating in celebrations and rituals with feasts and special foods. Significantly, children were personally aware of the inner life of the spirit, beautifully voiced by Benjamin, "My soul is a little ghost inside me."

If you ask a young child, "Where does God come from, and where does God live?" without hesitation and by intuition, she will tell you what she believes. She knows instinctively what she likes, who she loves, and who loves her. Through imagination, she enlivens her toys and pets in the visible world and animates the mysteries of the invisible world. She ascribes truths as she perceives them to fairy tales and stories of her own making. It is as if she transcends the veil between earth and heaven, similar to the mystics Hildegard of Bingen, Mother Julian of Norwich, and First Nations people.

In *Born Believers: The Science of Children's Religious Belief* (2012), Justin L. Barrett presents numerous experiments concerning natural beliefs of God with American, British, Greek, Israeli, Maya, and Spanish children. He writes, "Children come into the world with a tendency to see order, purpose, and even intentional design" (10). His studies indicate that development from infancy and early childhood is a sensitive period for language and music and that differences in the properties of physical objects and agents are perceived. "By agents, I mean to include people and any other beings we understand as not merely reacting to their environment but intentionally acting on it" (24). Barrett reasoned that children readily accept the presence of unseen agents, such as imaginary playmates, spirits, and gods.

> Hence, what children believe is restricted by their conceptual abilities, no matter how enthusiastically or forcefully enforced an idea is by parents. When it comes to religious beliefs, if the ideas are too counter-intuitive and thereby fall too far outside children's conceptual abilities, they will not be believed. On the other hand, concepts that are readily conceived of *and* fit with their naturally arising conceptual biases will be more likely to be believed.
>
> (192)

Our investigation of children's spirituality did not include interviews with pre-set questions; instead, we conducted field research on children's spontaneous responses in various settings. We collected vignettes and described them in artful narratives. Spiritual themes emerged from the children's activities and behaviors: pilgrimages, sojourners, faith traditions, spirit animals, found treasures, and sacred artifacts. Incidents, like threads, are woven into a story, a web, or a tapestry. The richness, complexity, and dimensionality of children's encounters with the visible and invisible, known and unknown, reveal new perspectives and understanding of the mystical child searching for meaning. Children's spiritual identity is expressed through purity of heart and qualities of goodness. Their openness to the truths of faith traditions and mysteries of nature is mysticism at its source and consciousness at its beginning.

> *Our birth is but a sleep and a forgetting:*
> *The soul that rises with us, our life's star,*
> *Hath had elsewhere its setting*
>   *and cometh from afar:*
> *Not in entire forgetfulness,*
>   *and not in utter nakedness,*
> *But trailing clouds of glory, do we come*
>   *from God, who is our home:*
> *Heaven lies about us in our infancy!*[1]

Note

1 William Wordsworth (1770–1850) "Intimations of Immortality" from *Recollections of Early Childhood* (1807, stanza 5).

References

Barrett, Justin L. *Born Believers: The Science of Children's Religious Belief*. Simon and Schuster, 2012.

Buller, Laura. *A Faith Like Mine: A Celebration of the World's Religions: Through the Eyes of Children*. Dorling Kindersley, 2005.

Wordsworth, William. "Intimations of Immortality." In: *Recollections of Early Childhood and Other Poems*. Houghton Mifflin, 1807.

9

Peace in Search of Makers

Danette Littleton

The Golden Rule is universal among people of all faiths and humanistic philosophies. The rule is a unifying message of living in peace and harmony. Jeffrey Wattles' *The Golden Rule* (1996) provides an extensive study of its history and ethics. He examined early texts by Confucius and discussed the emergence of the Golden Rule according to ancient Greeks and Romans. Rabbi Hillel asserted that by the first century, the Golden Rule summarized the Torah. New Testament Gospel writers Matthew and Luke sought interpretations of the rule against a social background of reciprocity and retaliation. Theologians during the Middle Ages, Augustine, Aquinas, Luther, and others, embraced the Golden Rule in their theology.

The remaining chapters of Wattles' book refer to the rule in literature, dating from early through modern eras. In the twentieth century, the rule appeared in theories of human development, such as those of Jean Piaget, Lawrence Kohlberg, Erik Erikson, and others (11). Wattles writes, "Part II [in the book] sets forth a philosophical and religious context for the complete practice of the rule. The resulting ethics honors morality, sharpens intuition through moral thinking, acknowledges the complex social context of interaction, and leads the practitioner beyond duty-conscious rule-following to loving spontaneity" (12).

Children, too, embody the Golden Rule in thought, word, and deed.

Meira protects a little fish from harm with kindness and care.

Shaka:	"We can take care of each other." *Walking School Bus*.
Zoe:	"Chants for the happiness of others." Buddhist. United States.
Maiko:	"Be aware of ourselves and to review our attitudes again and again." Buddhist. Japan.
Benjamin:	"My faith allows me to get in touch with my soul." Jewish. France.
Antonio:	"We love and forgive each other." Christian. Italy.
Hannah:	"We listen [to the preacher] and try to do good so that our faith will help us every day." Christian. Ghana.
Rachid:	"How to be good with people and behave in a nice way." Islam. Morocco.
Mohammed:	"My faith makes me feel peaceful and secure." Islam. Dubai.

In *Journey to Japan*, Meira, her mother, and her sister immerse themselves in Planets, an interactive exhibit enabling them to become one with the world.

At another museum exhibit, Falling Flowers, Meira ponders for a long time and tells her mother, "This is about life, being born, growing, and dying. The different colored flowers are the different personalities that make each person special."

"The golden rule and its consequences: A practical and effective solution to world peace," Zahra Rakhshani (2017) gives evidence that the golden rule is universal across the world's religions.

Bahá'í Faith
Lay not on any soul a load that you would not wish to be laid upon you, and desire not for anyone the things you would not desire for yourself. *Bahá'u'lláh*, **Gleaning**

Buddhism
Treat not others in ways that you yourself would find hurtful.
The Buddha, **Udana-Varga 5.18**

Christianity
In everything, do to others as you would have them do to you; for this is the law and the prophets.
Jesus, **Matthew 7:12**

Confucianism
One word which sums up the basis of all good conduct is loving-kindness. Do not do to others what you do not want done to yourself.
Confucius, **Analects 15.23**

Hinduism
This is the sum of duty: do not do to others what would cause pain if done to you.
Mahabharata 5:1517

Islam
Not one of you truly believes until you wish for others what you wish for yourself. *The Prophet Muhammad,* **Hadith**

Jainism
One should treat all creatures in the world as one would like to be treated.
Mahavira, **Sutrakritanga 1.11.33**

Judaism
What is hateful to you, do not do to your neighbour. This is the whole Torah; all the rest is commentary. Go and learn it.
Hillel, **Talmud, Shabbat 31a**

Native Spirituality
We are as much alive as we keep the earth alive.
Chief Dan George

Taoism
Regard your neighbour's gain as your own gain and your neighbour's loss as your own loss
Lao Tzu, **T'ai Shang Kan Ying P'ien, 213–218**

Unitarianism
We affirm and promote respect for the interdependent web of all existence of which we are a part.
Unitarian principle

Zoroastrianism
Do not do unto others whatever is injurious to yourself.
Shayast-na-Shayast 13.29

The teachings of Jesus of Nazareth in the Sermon on the Mount signify the tenets of the Golden Rule, Matthew 5:2–12, The Beatitudes (3–9):

> [3] "Blessed are the poor in spirit, for theirs is the kingdom of heaven.
> [4] "Blessed are those who mourn, for they shall be comforted.
> [5] "Blessed are the meek, for they shall inherit the earth.
> [6] "Blessed are those who hunger and thirst for righteousness, for they shall be satisfied.
> [7] "Blessed are the merciful, for they shall receive mercy.
> [8] "Blessed are the pure in heart, for they shall see God.
> [9] "Blessed are the peacemakers, for they shall be called the sons of God.

In conclusion, Wattles suggests, "[The] human compacity to participate in the spiritual presence of Jesus [goes beyond] the instruction available in rational principles [to gain] spiritual strength and divine wisdom [in] the practice of the golden rule" (161). The presence of the sacred resides in our spiritual interactions, "Do unto others as you want others to do unto you." Wattles reasons that a spiritual interpretation of the rule enables communities to grow and flourish. "The experience of love is an actual community [...] of humanity divinely united" (159, 160).

The Golden Rule is simple and accessible to everyone, with or without a religious affiliation or belief. If we practiced kinship, there would be goodwill in our communities, towns, cities, and nations. However, there are unyielding hindrances and obstructions to peace, locally and globally. Modern societies are being split into hostile factions, *us and them*. Countless people are displaced due to excessive heat, drought, floods, wildfires, and epic storms. Relentless wars render innocent people helpless and suffering as their homes and cities are destroyed. Before we yield to despair and defeat, there is reason for hope. With each birth, life begins afresh as the infant seeks to belong, love, and be loved: hope is born.

Emily Dickinson (2019) tells us that hope, although mysterious, is eternal:

> "Hope" is the thing with feathers –
> That perches in the soul –
> And sings the tune without the words –
> And never stops – at all –
>
> And sweetest – in the Gale – is heard –
> And sore must be the storm –
> That could abash the little Bird
> That kept so many warm –
>
> I've heard it in the chilliest land –
> And on the strangest Sea –
> Yet – never – in Extremity,
> It asked a crumb – of me.

In seeking the mystical child, we observed, recorded, transcribed, and analyzed children's spontaneous activities, behaviors, and comments in various settings. We also researched the lives of medieval mystics, beliefs across world religions, children's faith traditions, and the universality of the Golden Rule. The next chapter will focus on acknowledging and understanding God through the great religions and their origins.

References

Dickinson, Emily. *Hope Is the Thing with Feathers: Poems of Emily Dickinson*. Gibbs Smith, 2019.

Rakhshani, Zahra. "The golden rule and its consequences: A practical and effective solution for world peace." *Journal of History Culture and Art Research*, 6.1, 2017, pp. 465–473.

Wattles, Jeffrey. *The Golden Rule*. Oxford University Press, 1996.

10

Seeking God

Danette Littleton

In *God: A Human History* (2017), Reza Aslan seeks God and the divine in human history and its origins. He writes that while we don't know where the idea of the soul comes from, "What seems clear, however, is that the belief in the soul may be humanity's *first* belief. Indeed, if the cognitive theory of religion is correct, belief in the soul is what led to belief in God" (47). A universal belief in the existence of the soul led to a belief in a divine presence. That belief was

> personalized, given names and backstories, endowed with human traits and emotions, and cast into a thousand different forms, each with its own personality and purpose; and how after many years and with great difficulty, those forms gave way to a single divine personality we know today as God.
>
> (47)

In this elegant and insightful book, Aslan recounts his spiritual life through faith traditions and scholarship, as he says, or a combination of the two, in search of a distinction between God and himself. He concludes that there is no separation. "I am, in my essential reality, God made manifest. We all are" (169). He states that he is a believer and pantheist who believes that reality, the universe, and nature are an immanent deity that, from the beginning of time, continues to create. "I recognize the divinity of the world and every being in it as though they were God—because they are. And I understand the only way I can truly know God is by relying on the only thing I can truly know—*myself*" (169). Aslan does not proselytize; instead, he suggests—believing in God or not—defining God in your way is your choice (171).

From a different perspective, Rodney Stark, in *Discovering God: The Origins of the Great Religions and the Evolution of Belief* (2007), studied the history of religion through its particular roles and institutions. In this work, he takes the reader on a guided spiritual tour through time from primitive societies of the Stone Age to the first stop at Sumer, "a collection of city-states located around the lower Tigris and Euphrates Rivers" (64).

At the first light of civilization, it is said that history begins at Sumer. Thomas Cahill, in *The Gift of the Jews* (1998), wrote that just before the invention of written language, an explosion of technological creativity in Sumer would not be matched until the nineteenth and twentieth centuries, not only in agriculture but also in "wheeled transport, sailing ships, metallurgy, and wheel-turned oven-baked pottery" (13). Moreover, the Sumerians were the first to "erect vastly impressive, even overwhelming enclosures for business and ritual: monumental stone sculpture, engravings, and inlay, the brick mold, the arch, the vault, and the dome all first came to light under the dazzling Sumerian sun" (13).

Sumerians produced "thousands of [hardened clay] tablets inscribed in cuneiform scripts [found in] spectacular ruins, artifacts, frescoes, and carvings from which we have our earliest information about *organized* religion." Sumerians' religion comprised "specialized priesthoods, elaborate rites, written scriptures, and a multitude of Gods," all housed in great structures" (Stark, 64). In contrast, Old World sacred texts of Egypt, Greece, and Rome did not survive since they were primarily written on perishable materials, such as papyrus or leather. In contrast, Stark points out that cultures of the New World's sacred writings and artworks are well-preserved, such as Aztec pictographs, Mayan glyphs, and Inca *Khipu* discovered in great temples and caves.

In Egyptian history, Amenhotep IV (1379 BCE) abandoned Egypt's ancient polytheistic religions and established one God, Aten, the God of Egypt. He changed his name to Akhenaten, meaning the glorious spirit of Aten. He proclaimed that One God ruled over all other deities and commanded eliminating all names, images, and references to the old gods. In a *Great Hymn*, Akhenaten proclaimed, "There is no other who knows thee save thy son Akhenaten. Thou hast made him wise in thy plans and thy power" (Stark, 158). Akhenaten's attempt to establish monotheism failed dramatically because he ignored the need for more than one follower and believer—himself. "Atenism" may be characterized as less monotheistic and more monarchical. After he died, the new Pharoh restored the old religion, its gods, shrines, and priests (Stark, 161). The monotheism of the Hebrew Bible had a separate development that began more than half a millennium after the pharaoh's death when Egypt returned to a plurality of gods. Thus, Judaism is the world's oldest and most continuous monotheistic religion. Words first recorded: "In the beginning, God created."

I saved Thomas Cahill's subheading of his book *The Gift of the Jews* for just this moment in my text: *How a Tribe of Desert Nomads Changed the Way Everyone Thinks and Feels*. In just a few words, Cahill called attention to the ancient history, culture, written and oral traditions, and religion of a people who changed the world.

> Without the Jews, we would see the world with different eyes, hear with different ears, and feel with different feelings. [...] the role of the Jews, the inventors of Western culture, is singular: there is simply no one else even remotely like them.
>
> (3)

Hear, O Israel, the Lord Our God, The Lord is One.

Judaism, a *religion of the book*, distinguishes itself from other scriptures of the time. The Tanakh (known by Christians as the Old Testament) consists of the Torah (the first five books of Moses), the writings of the prophets, the Psalms, and other writings that tell the history of the Israelites and the relationship between Israel and God (Stark, 170).

Yaakov Ariel, a scholar of Jewish–Christian relationships and new Jewish religious movements, wrote a brief yet comprehensive essay, "A Faith Worth Preserving: An Introduction to Judaism" (2005). In it, he cites archeological evidence of the Israelite community from around the 13th century BCE. He introduces sacred scriptures: the Torah, the Covenant between God and Abraham, King David and King Solomon, rebuilding Jerusalem as a center of Judaism, the Sabbath, and holiday celebrations.

> For many Jews, Judaism is much more than a faith—it is a community of people sharing the same rituals and celebrations, the same past, the same collective memories, and the same historical narrative. They are all heirs to a people who have refused to assimilate and have retained their faith and norms, facing, at times, persecution.
>
> (38)

For out of Zion shall go forth the law and the word of the Lord from Jerusalem.

(Isaiah 2:2–3)

In his writing "In Search of Jewish Identity" (2016), Sir Jonathan Sacks, Chief Rabbi of the United Congregation of Great Britain and the Commonwealth, wrote,

> What are we? What makes us Jewish? This has been one of the persisting debates about Jewish life ever since the nineteenth century. Until then, people, by and large, knew who and what Jews were. They were the heirs of an ancient nation who, long ago, made a covenant with God in the Sinai desert and, with greater or lesser success, tried to live by it ever since. They were [and are] God's people.

In *Our Father Abraham: Jewish Roots of the Christian Faith*, Marvin Wilson (2021) suggests that a personal understanding of their faith's Jewish roots and Jerusalem's significance are essential for

Christians. The Apostle Paul, in a letter to the Romans, reminded early Christian followers: "Consider this: You do not support the root; the root supports you" (Romans 11:18b). Christianity's defining message is simple: *Love Your Neighbor as Yourself*. From its Jewish heritage, Christianity grew from the Hebrew Covenant with God to espouse a New Covenant. Jesus' life and teachings are recorded in the books of the New Testament, including the Gospels, Epistles, and other writings that portray Jesus as the Christ or Messiah (Bowker, 1997, 136). Jesus' knowledge of the importance of the sacred texts of the Five Books of Moses is evident in the Gospel of Matthew: *Do not imagine that I have come to abolish the Torah or the Prophets: I have come not to abolish but to complete* (Matthew 5:17–48).

Prophetically, Jesus asked his disciples, *Who do people say that I am?* His complex question remains as relevant today as when Jesus posed it, particularly among Biblical scholars, theologians, clergy, believers, non-believers, historians, archeologists, and the third President of the United States. Thomas Jefferson, who abstained from religious affiliation, personally or for the nation, set out his answer in a book. In 1820, Jefferson, at seventy-seven years of age, completed a project he'd long worked on, *The Life and Morals of Jesus of Nazareth, Extracted Textually from the Gospels in Greek, Latin, French & English*. Jefferson studied each translation of the Gospels, and, with a cut-and-paste strategy, he placed the translations side-by-side on each page of his book. Thus, he sought to clarify and refine Jesus' teachings to reveal "the most sublime and benevolent code of morals which has ever been offered to man." Jefferson proposed to purge the Gospels of the messages that seemed to him "contrary to reason," leaving only the "authentic" story of Jesus (*The Jefferson Bible*, Smithsonian Edition, 2011).

There is another profound rendering of the story of Jesus by the conversion of enslaved Africans. Henry Louis Gates, Jr., in *The Black Church: This is Our Story, This is Our Song* (2021), gives an extensive account of a people's story of faith from slavery to freedom. Gates writes, "It is the Black Church where the language of music and the music of language meet to create one grand, inimitable, irresistibly powerful form" (8). A one-of-a-kind repertory of songs emerged from African rhythmic, melodic, and improvised spontaneous singing and fused with Protestant hymns and stories from the King James Bible. These are among my favorites.

Songs of Sorrow: *No More Auction Block for Me, Sometimes I Feel Like a Motherless Child, Nobody Knows De Trouble I've Seen, I've Been 'Buked-I've Been Scorned, Wade in the Water.*

Songs of Going Home and Escape: *I'm Going Up Home Soon in the Morning, Going Over on the Other Side of Jordan, I Am Bound for Sweet Canaan's Happy Land, On Jordan's Stormy Banks I Stand.*

The Underground Railroad: *Follow the Drinkin' Gourd, De Gospel Train, Swing Low Sweet Chariot.*

Jubilee Songs: *Rocka My-Soul in the Bosom of Abraham, In That Great Gettin'-Up Morning, My Lord What a Morning.*

Songs of Bible Stories: *Little David Play on Your Harp, Didn't My Lord Deliver Daniel, The Old Ark a-Movering Along, Open the Window, Noah, Keep Your Lamps Trimmed and Burning.*

These, and many other spirituals and work songs are testimonies of an unnamable tragedy that divided families, of their unbearable needs and wants, and the hardship of daily life. The ultimate devastation of enslavement was the assault on heart, mind, soul, and body, and yet the people were sustained by hope and faith. There is nothing more telling than the songs they sang about the Israelites' escape from slavery in Egypt. Songs of escape (or planned escape) would bring punishment should the slaveholders or overseers hear and understand their secret messages. *Go Down* Moses is one of many such songs with hidden messages.

> Go down Moses
> Way down in Egypt land
> Tell old Pharaoh
> To let my people go!

> Oh, when Israel was in Egypt land
> Let my people go!
> Oppressed so hard, they could not stand
> Let my people go!

So, the Lord said, go down Moses
Way down in Egypt land
Tell old Pharaoh
To let my people go

So, Moses went to Egypt land
Let my people go!
He made old Pharaoh understand
Let my people go!

Yes, the Lord said, go down Moses
Way down in Egypt land
Tell old Pharaoh
To let my people go

Thus spoke the Lord, bold Moses said
Let my people go!
If not I'll smite your firstborn dead
Let my people go!

God the Lord said, go down Moses
Way down in Egypt land
Tell old Pharaoh
To let my people go!

Way down in Egypt land
Tell old Pharaoh
To let my people go

In *No god but God: The Origins, Evolution, and Future of Islam* (2011), Reza Aslan begins, "A story anchored in the memories of the first generation of Muslims and cataloged by the Prophet Muhammad's earliest biographers" that reveals […} the ideology of the Muslim faith in its infancy: that is, "before the faith became a religion before the religion became an institution" (xxiv). This story of faith began fourteen centuries ago with Muhammad ibn Abdallah's birth in Mecca. He became known as The Prophet and Messenger of God. Aslan explains,

> This book is not just a critical reexamination of the origins and evolution of Islam, nor is it merely an account of the current struggle among Muslims to define the future of this magnificent and misunderstood faith—[it] is, above all else, an argument for reform.
>
> (xxvi)

Less known (except for scholars) are Muhammad's beliefs regarding Jews and Christians of his time. "The Qur'an, as a holy and revered scripture, repeatedly reminds Muslims that what they are hearing is not a new message but the confirmation of previous scriptures (100).

Tragically, after 1400 years, this understanding among the great faiths of Abraham—Judaism, Christianity, and Islam—no longer prevails. The complexity of Islam's history and religion are far too complex to describe here. In subsequent chapters, through extensive notes and references, Aslan submits a detailed, historical, and chronological account of the oppression of colonialism, divisive factions, internal disputes, both religious and aggressive, and the tragedy of September 11th and its repercussions. Still, Aslan offers hope for the future of Islam.

> It may be too early to speculate about how the sense of radical individualism and anti-institutionalism that has seized Muslims across the world will influence Islam in the coming years. [...] The next chapter in the story of Islam will be written solely by those willing to look forward to confronting whatever lies ahead. [...] Rather, it is solely through the slow and steady building of personal relationships that one discovers the fundamental truth that all people everywhere have the same dreams and aspirations and that all people struggle with the same fears and anxieties. [...] That day will come. Perhaps then we will recognize the intimate connections that bind us all together beyond any cultural, ethnic, or religious affiliations.
>
> (292)

> *Inshallah.* God willing.
>
> (xv)

This tour through Judaism, Christianity, and Islam ends here for the brevity of text without disregarding the many other great religions of the world, such as Zoroastrianism, Hinduism, Buddhism, Chinese Folk Religion, Taoism, Confucianism, Sikhism, Shinto, and Native Religions.

Previously, we have referred to God but abstained from defining *God*. That is to say, we respect each individual's relationship and understanding of God(s), beginning with the people of the first light and you, our readers.

Chapter Notes

The Khipu are knotted-string devices used to collect data and record statistical and narrative data.

National Geographic explorer and engineer Albert Lin unearths and brings images and artifacts of Inca and Mayan civilizations to life: *Lost Cities with Albert Lin*—TV documentaries.[1]

Recommended video recordings:

Let My People Go. Paul Robeson
   https://youtu.be/gtLcELU1brA?si=FRCcJhU_8rN9lTt7
No More Auction Block for Me. Odetta
   https://youtu.be/AHVWpcJsZBw?si=p9cTrzOhvMuMRtj
On Jordan's Stormy Banks I Stand. Riverside Ghanaian SDA Church Choir
   https://youtu.be/cyFwMVkZGrs?si=mi6NzJrwIIzlQ9yj
Keep Your Lamps Trimmed and Burning. Andre J. Thomas and Zbor sv. Nikolaja Litija Choir.
   https://youtu.be/1XuR5oh_4iE?si=n2JJ59P5gNENHwHc
Revelations, The Alvin Ailey American Dance Theater, choreographer, Alvin Ailey.
Celebrating Six Decades of *Revelations*, Lincoln Center, 2015.
   https://youtu.be/kDXerubF4I4?si=w8-8UAz4b9xu3sjj
The Music of Revelations: The Alvin Ailey American Dance Theater. The Alvin Ailey Dance Foundation, Inc., 1998.
"Portrait of Ailey, A New Eight-Part documentary series available for free on PBS Learningmedia: Educational materials

accompanying the series encourage students to explore the perpetual power of dance."
https://s3.amazonaws.com/cms.ipressroom.com/292/files/20241/Portrait+of+Ailey+x+PBS+LearningMedia_Final.pdf

Note

1 The book Umm al-Kitab, or "Mother of Books," is found among pre-Islamic Persians, indicating Islamic monotheism.
    Friedman, Yaron (2010). *The Nuṣayrī-ʿAlawīs: An Introduction to the Religion, History and Identity of the Leading Minority in Syria*. Islamic History and Civilization. Vol. 77. Leiden: Brill.

References

Ariel, Yaakov, A Faith Worth Preserving: An Introduction to Judaism in Hughes, Amanda Milly. *Five Voices Five Faiths: An Interfaith Primer*. Cowley Publications, 2005.

Aslan, Reza. *No god but God: The Origins, Evolution, and Future of Islam*. Random House, 2011.

Aslan, Reza. *God: A Human History*. Random House, 2017.

Bowker, John. *World Religions: The Great Faiths Explored and Explained*, Dorling Kindersley, 1997.

Cahill, Thomas. *The Gift of the Jews: How a Tribe of Desert Nomads Changed the Way Everyone Thinks and Feels*. Doubleday, 1998.

Gates, Henry Louis, Jr. *The Black Church: This is Our Story, This is Our Song*. Penguin Press, 2021.

Sacks, Jonathan. "In Search of Jewish Identity: Kedoshim: Covenant & Conversation." *The Rabbi Sacks Legacy*, The Rabbi Sacks Legacy, 6 Sept. 2016, http://rabbisacks.org/covenant-conversation/kedoshim/in-search-of-jewish-identity/

Stark, Rodney. *Discovering God: The Origins of the Great Religions and the Evolution of Beliefs*. Harper One, 2007.

Wilson, Marvin R. *Our Father Abraham: Jewish Roots of the Christian Faith*. Eerdmans Publishers, (2021).

11

The Mystery of God

Danette Littleton and Meryl Sole

In the beginning, I was merely an infant, heartbroken in my isolation. In truth, I was trying to find my way home. I cannot say how long I wandered aimlessly through the dark of time. I walked for miles and miles, stumbling in the dark, trembling with loneliness; then, I finally stood still in the vast blackness and let out a cry. I saw that cry rise like an arrow, reaching the center of the heavens and exploding into fragments that became stars. Where my cry had fallen stood a solitary burning ball. My shards of light had created a gigantic spatial metropolis in which I began to look for a place to live.

In this fictional account, *The Life of God (As Told by Himself)*, Franco Ferrucci (1996) imagines that God is lonely until he falls in love with Earth. God plunges into the oceans and lives as a plant, a reptile, and a bird. Centuries pass, and God has long talks with Moses, engages with Greek philosophers, becomes friends with Buddha, and attends the birth of Jesus. God also meets scientists, theologians, and mystics and loves his friend Mozart's playfulness and his music. But, over time, God feels out of place with his creation. At the end of his memoir, God is packing his bags.

What does it mean if God is disappointed with his children? Is God weeping at our stewardship of his creation? Is God saddened by the scars of wars and human suffering? I think it means that God is *seeking* us to come home. When we show compassion and kindness to others, God radiates through us. We embody God's presence when we express love for our children, partners, families, and friends. We manifest God's purpose when we show others compassion, justice, dignity, and fairness. Mother Theresa tells us, "… God and compassion are one and the same" (p. 179).

For the Love of God (Carson, 2006) is a collection of essays by acclaimed teachers, thinkers, and philosophers in which they examine their relationships with the divine. These relationships are at the core of all religious teachings. Author and lecturer Marianne Williamson shares, "Our relationship with God is our relationship with ourselves because the divine in us is who we essentially are" (xv). Many of the personal accounts in this collection begin with references to childhood connections to God.

Priest, theologian, and author Matthew Fox describes a relationship with God that began in childhood when he contracted polio and miraculously recovered. As a young child, Fox was filled with gratitude that still lies at the heart of his spirituality. A connection to his childhood provides wisdom for walking a path with God. Fox shares, "…we can learn to delight again and to play again, then we can learn wisdom again. That's how we accompany God through our journey and through his universe" (p. 15).

Howard Murphet, an author and devotee of Indian spiritual master Sai Baba, writes about an early profound relationship with God that continued to transform from childhood. Higher education caused the connection to disappear, but, through studies with a spiritual teacher, he was able to find his way back to the childhood connection, which now provides him with spiritual nourishment and understanding.

Brook Medicine Eagle, an American author, singer, and interpreter of Native American religions, shares a relationship with God that developed at an early age growing up on a remote ranch in the wilderness. As a child, her experience of God was through nature, mountains, and animals, laying a foundation for her lifelong connection to the Great Spirit.

Marsha Sinetar writes about her childhood, a time filled with curiosity and wonder, when family members stimulated her interest in examining big questions about God and faith. Her grandmother, "an active spiritual instigator" (p. 159), accompanied her. Sinetar concludes by describing her current relationship with a down-to-earth God who continues to speak to her through acts of love.

Perhaps these essays about the God of love—the great mystery of our essence, universal love, peace, compassion, and tolerance—resonate with you. You may also seek to learn more about the relationship between science and religion. Over centuries, theologians, historians, physicists, and laypeople have considered the matter one of conflict and hostility or harmony and collaboration, yet others have regarded the relationship as entirely separate. Extensive studies by the Pew Research Center reveal no single, universally held view. It all depends on whom you ask about their thoughts concerning the intersection of scientific thought and spirituality.

In "Speaking of Faith," a series of public radio programs, award-winning broadcaster, journalist, and author Krista Tippett interviewed and discussed science and spirituality with physicists, psychologists, educators, and theologians. In 2010, Tippett published a collection of these broadcasts in *Einstein's God: Conversations about Science and the Human Spirit*. She engaged her guests in an intellectual dialogue about the interplay between science and religion. Tippett asserted that the either–or debate is not only unwinnable but misleading. The depth of thought presented in these essays can only be fully understood by reading each in total.

In the first chapter, Tippett discusses "Einstein's God" with physicist Freeman Dyson and astrophysicist Paul Davies. She writes, "Throughout his life, [Einstein] thrilled to all he could not yet understand. He was more than content with what he called a cosmic religious sense—animated by 'inklings' and 'wonderings' rather than by answers and conclusions" (16). In the spirit of this cosmic sensibility, Einstein found symbiosis in the prophets and psalmists of the Hebrew Bible, St. Francis of Assisi, and the Buddha. Einstein wrote,

> The religious geniuses of all ages have been distinguished by this kind of religious feeling. In my view, it is the most

important function of art and science to awaken this feeling and keep it alive in those who are receptive to it (33). His spirituality is best recognized in his love of music. "If I had not been a physicist, I would have been a musician." As a young boy, he studied the violin and played throughout his lifetime. "I often think about music. I daydream about music. I see my life in the form of music" (28).

Dear Professor Einstein: Letters to and From Children (2002) is a delightful little book that introduces Einstein through a short biography, a picture gallery, and letters from children and his replies. Children wrote to him as a personal friend, in awe of his work and "celebrity," with invitations to visit their school and requests for autographs. They ask funny questions, "I think you ought to have a haircut so you can look better," and profound ones, "Do scientists pray?" His replies were, at times, scientific, humorous, and loving, but always honest.

From Phyllis, New York, The Riverside Church, January 19, 1936 (2002, 128–129).

> *My dear Dr. Einstein,*
>
> *We have brought up the question: Do scientists pray? in our Sunday School class. It began by asking whether we could believe in both science and religion.*
>
> *[…] We will feel greatly honored if you will answer our question: Do scientists pray and what do they pray for?*
>
> *We are in the sixth grade, Miss Ellis's class.*
>
> *Respectfully yours,*
Phyllis

To Phyllis, New York, January 24, 1936

> *Dear Phyllis,*
>
> *I will attempt to reply to your question as simply as I can. Here is my answer:*
>
> *Scientists believe that every occurrence, including the affairs of human beings, is due to the laws of nature. Therefore, a scientist cannot be inclined to believe that the course of events*

can be influenced by prayer, that is, by a supernaturally manifested wish.

However, we must concede that our actual knowledge of these forces is imperfect so that, in the end, the belief in the existence of a final, ultimate spirit rests on a kind of faith. Such belief remains widespread even with the current achievements in science.

But also, everyone who is seriously involved in the pursuit of science becomes convinced that some spirit is manifest in the laws of the universe, one that is vastly superior to that of man. In this way, the pursuit of science leads to a religious feeling of a special sort, which is surely quite different from the religiosity of someone more naive.

With cordial greetings,
your A. Einstein

To Barbara, Washington, D.C., January 7, 1943, (2002, 140).

...Do not worry about your difficulties in mathematics; I can assure you that mine are still greater.

To his son Hans Albert, Einstein gave advice reflecting his thoughts on learning.
November 4, 1915. This is an excerpt (2002, 146):

Dear Albert,
Yesterday I received your sweet little letter, and it made me very happy ...
I'm very glad that you enjoy playing the piano ... play mainly the things that you enjoy, even if your teacher doesn't assign them to you. You learn most from the things that you enjoy doing so much that you don't even notice the time passing.
Kisses to you and Tete (Eduard, second son)

from your
Papa

In an essay titled "A Memorable Day," a child wrote about meeting Professor Einstein at Princeton in 1949 (2002, 170):

As the moment finally came, I began to get scared. I did not know how to act in front of a celebrity. But after he got talking to us, I lost all my fear because I knew he liked children.

Our purpose in presenting selected viewpoints on how people think about God is to reveal, know, and nurture children's spirituality. To those who say, "I am not religious," we say that it matters less—about telling your children about religion or sending them to church, synagogue, mosque, or other house of worship—than sharing the awe and wonder of the natural world and the Oneness of the universal family. Believers and non-believers can share in the spirit of children's imaginative responses to ways they experience the seen and unseen, known and unknown worlds.

As spiritual guides, children help us see the sacred through their eyes and recall our childhood innocence and purity of heart. Listen, watch, wait, and affirm with open hearts and minds. Let children lead.

References

Calaprice, Alice, Editor. *Dear Professor Einstein: Albert Einstein's Letters to and from Children.* MJF Books, 2002.

Carson, Donald Arthur. *For the Love of God (Vol. 2): A Daily Companion for Discovering the Riches of God's Word.* Crossway, 2006.

Ferrucci, Franco. *The Life of God (as Told by Himself).* University of Chicago Press, 1996.

Tippett, Krista. *Einstein's God: Conversations about science and the human spirit.* Penguin, 2010.

12

Spiritual Engagements

Activities and Experiences

Meryl Sole

In this chapter, I share practical applications for the concepts presented throughout our book. Many of the activities detailed below are projects I regularly share with my graduate students and young children. Try them out on your own, with others, or adapt them to suit children of any age.

Exploring Your Inner World

Read *Experiences, Reflections, and Insights: Reading, Writing, and Children's Inside Worlds* by educator and author Jeffrey Pflaum (2021). Consider how you might design an activity to encourage participants to engage with their "inner worlds." Adapt Pflaum's counting and music techniques to provide students with an opportunity to explore their "… minds and imagination's ability to observe, record, visualize, re-create, create, and reflect on images" (p. 3).

Responding to Music

Share a musical selection from our Spotify playlist (link in notes) of spiritual music and ask participants to "draw how the music feels." Share artwork with the group and look for similarities in represented themes. Discuss similarities and differences in the groups' responses with what we described in our pilot study for this book.

Childhood Memories of Awe

Over the past few years, I have interviewed and surveyed many adults about their childhood memories of awe; many recalled experiences in the grandeur of nature or at a music performance where they remembered profound feelings of wonder and amazement. Ask participants to consider their earliest childhood memories of a formative awe experience and use an artistic medium (poetry, photography, drawing, painting, written story, drama, musical composition, dance, etc.) to represent that experience. Provide a space to share artwork and reflect on how past experience impacts current expression and understanding.

Self-Discovery Poetry

Explore poetry as a medium for self-discovery and understanding by scaffolding poetry writing with "fill-in-the-blank poems." Search for online templates of "I am" and "I am from" poetry to explore identity, history, cultural/religious background, etc. Participants may read their poems to the group or share them on a bulletin board, giving space to discuss similarities, differences, and uniqueness of experiences.

Belonging to the Natural World

Find inspiration in nature and natural materials. Go outdoors on a magical scavenger hunt and collect rocks, sticks, leaves, shells, and other treasures. With the materials, participants can create collages, sculptures, or mosaics and consider the musical possibilities of these items. If weather permits, enhance the experience of making art and music outdoors in nature, finding more inspiration in the sights, sounds, and scents around you.

Intuition: Invisible Threads, Spiritual Mirrors

Dramatic movement activities are a great way to connect with others using nonverbal communication. In *Spiritual Mirrors*, participants select a partner and face that person as the music plays. Without speaking, each partner takes turns leading a movement mirrored by the other, trying to sync up so that observers cannot tell who is leading and who is following. The partners attempt to switch roles seamlessly, transferring energies and intentions to one another. In *Invisible Threads*, participants form a line at one end of the room, standing shoulder to shoulder, looking straight ahead, and not making eye contact. As music plays, the line attempts to walk as one, moving at the same pace as held together by an invisible thread. The line of participants tries to tap into a shared energy to synchronize pace and movement.

Patchworks and Portraits: Observing Children's Spirituality

Design a mini-research project where participants can complete fieldwork observations of children in natural settings and classrooms (secular and sacred) and compile field notes and additional data sources. Weave the observations together into artistic vignettes and share them with the group. Participants may wish to create drawings or paintings of the group's vignettes to assemble in a patchwork quilt of experiences to display.

Walking a Labyrinth

Access the Labyrinth Locator (https://labyrinthlocator.org/), a worldwide community resource that connects people to nearby labyrinths. As a group, arrange a field trip to a local labyrinth. Prepare for your visit using guidelines outlined in Artress's work, setting expectations for the experience, including limited verbal communication and possible background music. Based on age, participants can reflect on the experience of walking the labyrinth through written vignettes or drawings.

A Faith Like Yours

Explore Laura Buller's children's book *A Faith Like Mine*. Pretend you are contributing pages to the book and designing personal collages, including significant holiday and festival observances, religious artifacts, traditional foods, etc., representing your personal faith experience.

Children's Stories of Kinship and Goodwill across Culture and Faith

Explore current news stories about children of diverse backgrounds and faiths who engage in acts of kindness, empathy, and compassion. Consider using different artistic mediums to represent the stories. Participants can share headlines and summaries of their inspirational stories, and together, the group can paint or draw a shared mural.

Connecting with the Divine

Contemplate your relationship to the divine. Use art, music, dance, or written word to represent your personal faith journey. Consider creating a faith journey map to illustrate significant moments, challenges, and turning points in your spiritual life. Connect these moments through spiritual pathways.

Communal Resource List to Support Children's Spirituality

Contribute to a shared list of resources, including spiritually inspiring children's literature, music, art projects, videos, and activities.

Artistic Expression and Sacred Practice through Stories/Myths of Creation: A Multi-Session Workshop

Begin by examining a variety of children's books on creation stories and myths from diverse cultures and faith traditions. Break into small groups that each select their own children's book to guide participation in four separate units: 1. Drawing, Painting, and Sculpting Creation, 2. Composing and Performing a Soundtrack for Creation, 3. Dancing Creation, and 4. Dramatizing and Writing Creation. Consider a final performance at the end of the workshop that features an art gallery, musical, dance, and dramatic performances. Provide space for discussion and reflection.

The following activities come from my graduate students' classrooms.

Uncovering Natural Mysteries

My graduate student, Thomas Readett, shared an inspirational activity with his elementary school students. After completing an outdoor scavenger hunt, students returned to the classroom with their found treasures and participated in a collaborative art project. Students took turns hiding the mystery scavenger hunt items (leaves, twigs, bottlecaps, coins) for each other under large sheets of paper. Using crayons and chalk, each child rubbed their paper on top of the objects, revealing the mystery of the unique arrangements of the natural materials. Students were enchanted to "reveal the magic" left by their classmates.

Dramatic Play Exercises

Graduate student Katie Garcia shared an activity to explore sacred feelings in an imaginary, enchanted forest. In her classroom of three- and four-year-olds, Katie introduced magical music and began the drama in a scary part of the forest. The children moved around, using their movements to illustrate feeling scared, spooky, and mysterious. As the music transformed, Katie guided the children to explore emotions like calmness, courage, and strength. The children found expression through dancing, skipping, hopping, running, and creating various characters that interacted with each other. Together, the children crafted a theatrical drama using their bodies and words to shape and transform the story. As a theatre specialist deeply interested in children's spiritual expression, Katie provides space in her classroom to encourage dramatic play, emotional expression, musical exploration, and dance. She is also working on a puppet theater activity where her children craft their puppet characters and perform spontaneous shows together.

The Golden Mist Meditation

Graduate student Laura Gold shared that her interest in storytelling, creative writing, and meditation stemmed from her childhood. She designed a children's visualization meditation to support them in accessing their emotions, sense of beauty, and wonder in an enchanted forest. Consider telling your story; use words to paint a picture and develop your meditation. Please share it with others and encourage them to slip away into your inspired story world, connecting to their energy and emotions. Children can do the same. If they are younger, encourage them to collaborate and share enchanting ideas and stories that can be woven into a shared meditation.[1,2]

Notes

1 THE GOLDEN MIST by Laura Gold.

    Are you ready to go on a magical journey? Let's start by getting cozy. Stretch your arms and legs and let out any wiggles or squirmy feelings. Then, when you're ready, close your eyes gently and take a deep breath in through your nose and out through your mouth. If it feels good, let out a big yawn. This helps your body and mind feel calm and ready for the adventure ahead. Now imagine that you're entering an enchanted forest that will transform you and give you sparkly powers. Picture standing in the middle of this magical forest, surrounded by tall, shimmering trees. The air is sweet with the smell of flowers, and the ground beneath your feet is soft and warm. There's a gentle breeze that tickles your hair, and birds sing in the trees. Everything here is peaceful and full of wonder. You feel your feet sinking into the soft earth, like you're a tree growing from the ground, your roots stretching deep into the earth. You feel calm and strong, like you belong here, like you're part of the woods. You can even feel the earth's energy moving up through your feet, filling you with peace. Now imagine that from your head to your toes, there's mud all over you. While this might feel a little yucky, it's actually magical mud that has built up from all the things you've carried with you, like tiredness, worries, or any feelings you might have been holding onto. Some of the mud might be thin, like a light dusting, and some might be thick, like a big pile. It's okay! This mud is here for a reason—it's just holding onto some of your old energy, and it's time to wash it away with your magic. Picture a sparkling, golden mist of light shining above your head. This light is warm, like feeling the sun on your face. Slowly, this golden light begins to fall from the sky, gently misting over your head. It's like a shimmering waterfall of light that washes over your whole body—down your arms, your legs, your tummy, and all the way down to your toes. As the golden mist touches the mud, something amazing happens—the mud starts to melt away, gently washing off everything you don't need. Keep imagining the golden light washing over you again and again, moving from your head to your toes. If any spots feel like they need a little extra help, you can use your magical powers. Maybe you have special sparkling hands, and you can wave them over the spots where the mud is being stubborn. You might even pretend to use a magic wand or a golden brush to wipe the mud away. Once the mud is gone, you're left glowing with a bright, beautiful energy! You're now shining with the most amazing light, like a magical creature that can do anything. You feel strong and peaceful. And then something even more amazing starts to happen—as the last bit of mud disappears into the earth below you, it starts to sprout tiny colorful flowers under your feet. They're bursting with all the colors of the rainbow—purple, orange, pink, blue, yellow, and red. Each step you take leaves behind a trail of flowers, filled with beauty. Take a few steps and watch as the flowers grow even more, filling the forest with their colors. You feel so light and happy, like your whole body is full of sparkles! As you say "thank you and goodbye" to the enchanted forest and the golden mist, take a few deep breaths. Feel how grounded and centered you are. When you're ready, slowly open your eyes, and come back to the world. Remember, whenever you need to feel calm or light, you can come back to this special forest and wash away anything that's not helping you feel your best.

2 Please access our Spotify playlist here: https://open.spotify.com/playlist/1ZVP4y
MngQGgB7FCIYmdNB?si=HjpVc5ZZTDmmbhFLW83S2Q&pi=u-7GsDCjaBSuGC.

References

Pflaum, Jeffery. "Experiences, reflections, and insights: Reading, writing and children's inside worlds." *Academia: Letters*, July 2021, pp. 1–5.

13

Spiritual Sojourners

Danette Littleton and Meryl Sole

While sojourners have multiple meanings, our journey in writing this book, from concept to completion, signifies a pilgrimage we took together. Here, we offer a conversation about issues and themes that shaped our work. This is our story of spiritual transcendence, discernment, acquired knowledge, and understanding.

The following transcript from Zoom meetings has been edited for clarity and brevity.

Meryl: Good morning.
Danette: Lovely to see you.
Meryl: And you.
Danette: Here we are at the end of writing our second book.
Meryl: It's been quite a journey of collaboration and discovery.
Danette: Shall we begin with the origins of this book?
Meryl: When *Knowing the Children We Teach* was published, we felt we had more to say, especially about children's spirituality growing out of children's expressions of wonder and awe.
Danette: Yes. I recall that our working title was *The Wondering Child*. Our book evolved from concept to completion

in search of children's voices of spirituality. To better understand spirituality, we studied world religions and discovered how mysticism seemed to apply to children's experiences of the unknown.

Meryl: We discovered portraiture, tapestry, threads, and story quilts as organizational frameworks.

Danette: I recalled the Greek myth of Ariadne and the labyrinth from the opera *Ariadne auf Naxos*. Following Ariadne's Thread, we found references within references to ancient and modern documentation of the labyrinth and its spiritual meaning.

Meryl: Yes, in particular, Lauren Artress's beautiful book on the sacred path of the labyrinth inspired me to experience it. A quick Google search revealed the presence of a labyrinth previously unknown to me right in my hometown.

Danette: From the outset of writing this book, we've had meaningful conversations about our religious traditions, Jewish and Christian, which we called "two paths to one God."

Meryl: Listening to children and observing them in sacred and secular places, including natural settings, we witnessed spiritual dimensions of enchantment, awe, and wonder. Even when adults were present, we noted that children acted alone as if in a private world, thus adding to our understanding of the child's spiritual world.

Danette: Your fieldwork is central to understanding young children's spiritual experience. Those inquiries revealed young children's experience of spirituality as they engaged in music, dance, image, and story.

Meryl: We hope our book will be widely read, especially by graduate students studying research. In my classes, these strategies help students decide what to study,

	target relevant resources, identify the most appropriate research design, and develop a creative writing process.
Danette:	Our model of child-centered qualitative research honors the importance of the child's voice and has implications for teaching children from their perspective.
Meryl:	Is there anything else we should share with our readers?
Danette:	I think it's important to reveal our family origins of faith. While we practice different religious traditions, our individual journeys are similar. Two paths to the same God.
Meryl:	We invite you to consider your journey with the Divine and encourage you to craft your own story in any artistic medium that inspires you.
Danette:	What's next for us? Another book?
Meryl:	Our third!
Danette:	We have more to say and learn together.
Meryl:	Absolutely. May our journey continue hand in hand along the next path.

THE LIGHT OF GOD

by Meryl Sole

Our family of four gathers in the kitchen and lights the Sabbath candles. Together, we sing the blessings for the candles, the wine, and challah bread. My husband and I raise our hands above our daughters' heads and bless our children. Then we chant together, "*Sh'ma Yisrael Adonai Eloheinu Adonai Eḥad.*" My husband has made it our family tradition to sing the Sh'ma on Shabbat, the Friday evening Sabbath. While more observant Jews recite this prayer every morning and evening, we share this once a week in our home. It means, "Hear, O Israel: the LORD is our God, the LORD is One." We stand together, arms wrapped around each other, bathed in the warmth of the candles, as we cover our eyes and sing together. It's a solemn, calm moment that feels sacred and filled with love. It is a spiritual connection.

This typical Friday night in my home was anything but ordinary. I've battled the idea of God for as long as I can remember. The God of my childhood who on Yom Kippur would seal us in the Book of Life, determining who shall live and who shall die. The God in the Bible stories taught by religious schoolteachers: an angry God who would punish. Fear and guilt surrounding a God who was hard to please, rules of observance and kashrut, the discipline I could never commit. Throughout my life, I still attended services, shared holiday meals, and practiced rituals, many of which I did not understand the meaning behind. I was raised by parents who carried on the traditions and later a spouse and extended family who did the same.

I have spent a lifetime avoiding or denying God. But in the glow of the candles on that cold Friday winter night, I realized, in an instant, that God was with me the whole time.

God was beaming in my young daughters' eyes and my husband's arms. God was everywhere: inside each of us and all around us. My God manifested through love. The rituals and prayers were meant to bring us closer together. The laws of the Torah were meant to guide our behavior and show us how to teach our children.

On that night, I made the decision not to fear but instead to love my God.

WHERE LOVE IS FOUND, GOD IS PRESENT

by Danette Littleton

My Grandmother's love is the source of my belief in a universal God of love and goodness. From the cradle, her love has sustained and nourished me.

Grandmother grew up in a small town when, across the rural south, clergy from different Christian denominations rode from town to town to preach—they were called circuit-riders. As a young girl, Grandmother heard varying interpretations of the Bible often with conflicting dogma by ordained ministers and preachers. Curious and intelligent, she listened to their messages but relied on her Biblical knowledge and wisdom.

When I was a young child, she told me stories of the Israelites, God's chosen people, of Moses and David, Ruth and Naomi, Jesus and Paul, as if they were acquaintances. She taught me to love my neighbor as myself, to forgive as we want to be forgiven, to be kind (merciful) and fair (just), not only in words, but deeds. Grandmama took care of the sick and needy; delivered babies for Black women who had no access to doctors or medicine; and provided clothes and food for homeless men riding railroad cars in search of work. Grandmother's way of love passed to her youngest child, my mother and from her to me. They taught me that service is at the center of Christian life.

My Grandmother embodied the humble life of a servant. She was called to see the needs of others, to show compassion regardless of race or religion, and the courage to act. The Prophet Isaiah wrote, "And if you spend yourselves on behalf of the hungry and satisfy the needs of the oppressed, then your light will rise, and your night will become like the noonday." Many years afterword, the message remained intact: "Dear children, let us not love with words or speech but with actions and truth" (John 3:18, NIV).

My spirituality evolved through music as well as the Word. I grew up in a time when everybody I knew sang, housework singing, evening front porch singing, and Sunday morning singing. Songs like "The Sweet By and By," "Amazing Grace," "This Little Light of Mine," "Balm in Gilead," my Grandmother sang to me, I sang to my young daughter. Even now on a quiet warm summer evening, I hear her "high lonesome" voice washing over me in waves of comfort, solace, joy and love, always love.

This song[1] is for her, Ada Elizabeth Peak Martin.

Shall we gather at the river?
Where bright angel feet have trod
With its crystal tide forever
Flowing by the throne of God

>   Yes, we'll gather at the river
>   The beautiful, the beautiful river
>   Gather with the saints at the river
>   That flows by the throne of God

Soon we'll reach the shining river
Soon our pilgrimage will cease
Soon our happy hearts will quiver
With the melody of peace

>   Yes, we'll gather at the river
>   The beautiful, the beautiful river
>   Gather with the saints at the river
>   That flows by the throne of God

Note

1 Robert Lowry (1826-1899) was a poet and gospel song composer who wrote hundreds of religious songs. Perhaps his most beloved is "Shall We Gather at the River." American composer Aaron Copland included Lowry's song in *Fanfare for the Common Man*, and Copland created settings for voices. Lowry wrote "Shall We Gather at the River" in 1864 during a tragic heatwave and epidemic that claimed many lives. He envisioned a passage in the Book of Revelations 22:1–2. *Then the angel showed me the river of the water of life, as clear as crystal, flowing from the throne of God and of the Lamb down the middle of the great street of the city. On each side of the river stood the tree of life, bearing twelve crops of fruit, yielding its fruit every month. And the leaves of the tree are for the healing of the nations.* Aaron Copland, "Shall We Gather at the River," The Smith College Glee Club. https://youtu.be/Luk_tctBU18.

For Product Safety Concerns and Information please contact our EU representative GPSR@taylorandfrancis.com
Taylor & Francis Verlag GmbH, Kaufingerstraße 24, 80331 München, Germany

www.ingramcontent.com/pod-product-compliance
Lightning Source LLC
Chambersburg PA
CBHW070404240426
43661CB00056B/2527